Using Raymon Grace's t shift in my clients, family, and friends, and they notice it too. Their outlook becomes positive and they seem to move from feeling stuck to seeing possibility in their lives. It is truly amazing to me to see their resistance simply disappear. I am deeply grateful to Raymon for giving me techniques to help my clients heal and to achieve my personal goals as well.

—Mary Mulcahy M.S.W., psychotherapist in private practice 25 years in Glastonbury, Connecticut

Raymon Grace has convinced this skeptical MIT graduate that we can create miracles, and consciously or unconsciously, do so every day. His method is to have you do the work yourself. To directly experience the largely untapped power of the mind. He is the most recent in a series of teachers who have weaned me from my former rigid, materialistic way of thinking and opened up staggering vistas of opportunity. Don't let Raymon's unpretentious manner fool you; he is a master healer and teacher.

—Roger Burbridge, Ph.D., former professor and psychologist

I am Ross H. Sheets and have a B.S. degree in law enforcement and am working toward my master's degree in criminal justice. I have over 30 years of police experience and currently work as a police officer in the state of Virginia. During my professional career I have worked with Raymon Grace on numerous investigations where he was responsible for providing essential information that led to the arrest of serial killers, rapists, and murderers. He has been useful in finding missing children and providing information for the protection of agents and law enforcement officers in performing the dangerous duties that we perform. Raymon truly has a gift from the High Spirits of the Light and God. Raymon's intent is to help all living beings and the Earth that we live on. Raymon's heart and soul are pure, and mankind will benefit from his information and the works that he provides. I have personally witnessed Raymon's healing powers on the sick and injured and the power he has to heal those with mental illness. Raymon is a friend and a hero.

—Ross H. Sheets

Raymon Grace is a very effective healer and teacher. This book is filled with practical wisdom and techniques that anyone interested in healing and other mind phenomena can understand.

Raymon's love and desire to be of service to the Earth and humankind shines through on every page. Absorb all the knowledge in this book and your life will never be the same.

—Harold McCoy, healer; founder and director, Ozark Research Institute

THE
FUTURE IS
YOURS

True Stories about Dowsing,

Spontaneous Healing, Ghost Busting, and

the Incredible Power of the Mind

RAYMON GRACE

HAMPTON ROADS

Hampton Roads Publishing Company, Inc.
Charlottesville, VA 22906
Distributed by Red Wheel/Weiser, LLC
www.redwheelweiser.com

Sign up for our newsletter and special offers by going to
www.redwheelweiser.com/newsletter/.

ISBN: 978-1-57174-706-8
Library of Congress Cataloging-in-Publication Data
available upon request.

Printed on acid-free paper in the United States of America

EBM

10 9 8 7 6 5 4 3 2 1

Dedication

Over 30 years ago, I set out to help someone with a hearing loss. This was before I knew anything about healing. My efforts to achieve this goal have taken me down many roads. Many people have benefited from my efforts. The goal has not been reached, but if it weren't for her, I would not have started, and this book would not have been written. This is why this book is dedicated to Nancy Grace.

Table of Contents

Foreword

If you love good stories that bring delight and raise your spiritual awareness, this book will do exactly that. Stories can illustrate a point in an often delightful and sometimes humorous way, making the point easy to remember. Raymon shares these stories in such a way that you will feel you are experiencing them with him. Accompanying the stories is text that shares the ideas, wisdom, and instructions to help you apply what is being shared.

Raymon freely and openly shares the techniques he uses to adjust energies in beneficial ways: energies that may seem to influence the health of all manner of things, including the Earth and ourselves—changes that may sometimes look like miracles. When asked how all this works, he will remind us that perhaps all things are composed of energies of some form or another, even our thoughts. And if our thoughts are composed of the same energies that make up everything around us, then it may be possible to influence our present as well as our probable futures. He expands this and many other ideas throughout this book.

Raymon is sharing the wisdom he has gleaned from his experiences, observations, and from many friends—friends from both the spirit world and this physical world. Friends like Chief Two Trees, Rolling Thunder, Bill and Winnie, and many others. This book has a lot to do with how to take back and use our creative powers—powers that we have often inadvertently given away or not recognized. The prime purpose of this book is to help us improve our ability to beneficially affect our lives and the lives of others. A book that you can truly enjoy, as well as using the insights that it offers.

> —Walt Woods, past president and trustee of the American Society of Dowsers, charter member of the Ozark Research Institute (ORI), author of *Letter to Robin* and *Powers that Be.*

Introduction

This book is blunt, down to earth, and (with the exception of my usual ramblings) to the point. It may not be eloquent, and the Queen's English may be butchered severely. No apologies are made. It is written with the encouragement of my many friends whose names would fill the book, some in this life and some who have crossed over.

The purpose of this book is to get you, the reader, to *think*, to imagine what you could do if you had more mental abilities. Next is to convince you that you *do have* these abilities, you just have to cultivate and learn how to use them. With these abilities comes the responsibility to use what you have in a respectful manner to improve your life, your family, and your community. These abilities can also be used to heal the Earth and our environment, of which we are a product. If the Earth is sick, and we are part of the Earth, then can we be totally well?

It is the accumulation of stories, information, and experiences gathered on the path of life, a path that has led to many places and has been shared with interesting people. Among these people are some who are well known and some who are equally important, but not so well known.

We are all the sum total of our heritage and environment. We may be stuck with our heritage, but we can change our environment. We can do this by bringing into our environment the people with characteristics and knowledge that we would like for ourselves. Among those who have enriched my environment and deserve appreciation are Bill and Winnie Askin, Harold McCoy, Rolling Thunder, Chief Two Trees, Jose Silva, Evelyn Rattray, Walt Woods, Tom Brown, Jr., and a number of others. It is the knowledge of these people and of the spirit world that, if properly used, can help us change the energy around us and thereby our future.

Special thanks go to Jack Kestner, who first wrote about the work we do and was the motivation to transform me from a backwoods mountain man into a backwoods international speaker.

Thanks also to Suzanne Cole, who edited the first edition of this book and was responsible for my advanced dowsing manual, *Techniques That Work for Me.*

This edition is 50 percent larger than the original book. My brother, David; his wife, Leslie; and my wife, Nancy, have been most helpful with their suggestions in putting this book together. I doubt that it could have been finished without them.

Several people have written stories and letters telling how they have been helped by the information you will find within these pages. Their stories are recorded as they wrote them. I hope this will give you, the reader, the encouragement to realize:

The future really is yours—and you can do something about it!

1 Learning the Basics

Sally was telling me about her new job as office manager and the problems that came with it. One employee in particular, Alice, had gone out of her way to be disagreeable and turn other employees against Sally. Morale and cooperation were low and conditions defied management.

Sally and I hadn't gotten together in a while, but we had been friends for a long time and this was an opportunity to do her a favor.

"Sally," I said, "I've learned a few things since we visited the last time, and if you like, we'll see what we can do about your office."

She agreed, and I began using a method to get the information needed to correct the problem. It only took a few minutes and as I relayed the information to her, she nodded her head in agreement. The place was a disaster—low motivation, something draining everyone's energy, ill will—the list went on and on. It took a while longer to make the corrections. Then I asked Sally how long it would be before she had a chance to get the office staff together.

"This Thursday we have a staff meeting, and that is only two days away!" she exclaimed.

"Will you let me know how it goes?"

"Sure," she agreed.

On Friday she sent an e-mail saying that the level of cooperation and overall energy in the office and staff had changed remarkably. Even Alice had come to her and offered to be more cooperative. A week later, conditions were still improved, making her job easier and more enjoyable.

Now, Sally had taken part in some unusual experiences with me before and this was not a great surprise to her. But you folks reading this probably want to know how it happened. After all, affecting office conditions several hundred miles distant is not what most people do for an evening's entertainment.

Well, that is one of the things this book is about. I just have to throw in some stories to get your attention. If you can survive the first few pages of technical information, the rest is easy. Once you learn the basics, everything else is just another technique.

You Can Perform Miracles

Now, folks, this book is about many things, but foremost is *self-empowerment*. Many examples are given here to encourage you, and to illustrate what can be done. Most of these examples are written in the words of those who actually accomplished these feats. They, for the most part, are people like you. They didn't have all the answers any more than you and I do. They just believed in themselves enough to do something.

The bottom line is this: If you can relax your body and mind enough to focus your thoughts, and use vivid visualization, you can perform miracles.

Now, don't complicate it. So many people miss the whole picture because it is so simple. I'll say it again: If you can relax your body and mind enough to focus your thoughts, and use vivid visualization, you can perform miracles.

We live in a world that wants to complicate everything. Lecturers and writers use big words and complicated terms to make themselves appear superior. I know for a fact that some speakers dangle a tidbit of information in front of the audience and then withhold the rest of the information. This appears to give the speaker a sense of superiority. My goal is to present this information in a manner that can be understood by anyone of average intelligence. You will not need a dictionary to read this book, because I never use a long word if a short one will do the job.

The basic idea is this: The future is composed of thoughts not yet materialized. We have the choice to create our future or let it be created by our indecision. We have created our present by our thoughts, decisions, and actions, or by their absence. By the same method, or lack of it, we create our future. We have a choice of which future we create. There are probably infinite possible futures for us, all dependent upon our thoughts and actions.

If there is one single message for people who attend my classes, it is this. You are not just victims of the elements and politicians. You have a choice, but having a choice is of little benefit unless you exercise it!

At each speaking opportunity, I make a statement that is in most part quoted from my friend Chief Two Trees. It goes like this:

"People have given their health to their doctor, their money to their banker, their soul to their preacher or priest, their children to the school system, and in so doing, have lost the power to control their lives." After the applause dies down, it is followed by this: "People buy things they don't need, at prices they can't afford, with money they don't have, to impress someone who doesn't give a damn."

The Power of Thought

OK, now that we know we have a choice in creating our future, how do we go about it? Well, first we have to learn how to think and to add power to our thoughts. Thoughts are the first step of creativity. Probably most people's thoughts are so scattered and at the wrong brain frequency that they don't really amount to much outside their own mind and body. Under stress, the brain frequency speeds up and this causes the thoughts to lose power. It also causes the immune system to weaken, thereby making one more vulnerable to disease and germs.

It is common knowledge that stress isn't all that good for us, and that the opposite of stress is relaxation. Stress also hinders us from focusing our mind, and there is much more power in a focused mind than a scattered mind.

My friend Harold McCoy and I speak at most major dowsing societies across the country. Harold, the founder of the Ozark Research Institute, makes a most impressive talk on "The Power of a Focused Mind." He has used this power of mind to get the ticks and fleas out of his yard. He has also used it to stop an oil leak in his car, and in thousands of successful healings on people.

Let's explain it like this. Everything has a frequency, vibration, beat, or cycle. Pick whichever word you like best. The Earth goes around the sun every 365 days, 6 hours, and a few minutes. The moon goes around the Earth every 28 days. The leaves that fall to the Earth will decay and go back to the Earth, and the tree, if left undisturbed, will go back to the Earth. All things come from the Earth and will return to the Earth. This is a cycle of nature.

Our heart has a cycle also; it beats about 70 times a minute. Now this is all understood by everyone. What is not so much understood is that the brain also has a frequency, beat, or cycle. In our normal state during the day, our brain is emitting about 20 beats per second, which is what is called the beta frequency. The brain frequency is separated into four parts. Depending on whose research you choose to believe, the frequencies are something like this. From 0.5 to 3 is called delta, from 4 to 7 is called theta, from 8 to 14 is called alpha, and from 15 up is called beta.

According to my information, there is a band of energy around the earth that vibrates at 10 beats per second, and this is the energy in the king's chamber of the Great Pyramid. Some believe the pyramid was built the way it is to create the alpha frequency to allow healing for the pharaoh and his family—exposure to the alpha frequency seems to allow the body to correct a multitude of problems.

It also seems possible to be able to create an alpha frequency with our hands. I have heard of a group of Native Americans who would shake their hands over the body of a sick or injured person to create a healing condition. Apparently this method has been around for a while, but not well known.

We know from experience that by moving our hands rapidly around the head of a person with a headache, the headache will, in most cases, vanish. This method has been used for many years with great success and in many cases the headaches never return, even after several years. The same method can be applied to other parts of the body.

There are two sides of the brain—the right and left hemispheres—and it is believed that only about 10 percent of the population uses both sides of the brain at the same time. This is greatly simplifying it, but the left side is the logical side and the right is the creative side. All children use both sides, which is why children have such vivid imaginations.

Think for a moment. Do you still have the imagination that you had as a child? Probably not. Why? Because most people lose their ability to equally use both sides of their brain as the body physically matures. Can you get it back? Yes. How? Stay with me and keep reading.

One of the first things we need to do is to learn to reach a more powerful state of mind. If we were able to consciously lower our brain waves, we could improve our immune system and give more power to our thoughts. It would also help us to use both sides of our brain.

Imagination

So you might ask, what benefit is it to use both sides of our brain? It improves our imagination. And what is the benefit of that? Well, any time we improve our imagination, we improve everything else our mind can do. And how does that work? Everything that exists in the physical world must first exist in the nonphysical world, the spirit world, or thought form. (Pick whichever term you like.)

These boots I wear once covered a cow. Someone had to skin the cow and scrape off the hair, tan the hide, cut out the patterns, and sew them into a pair of boots. However, before the cowhide ever became a pair of boots, the thought of the boots had to exist in the bootmaker's mind.

Same thing with a pair of jeans. They once were a cotton plant. Someone had to pick the cotton, clean it, process it, spin it into thread, weave it into cloth, cut out the pattern, and sew it into a pair of jeans. First, the thought of jeans had to exist.

As was stated earlier, thoughts are the first step of creativity. The more imagination we have, the more possibilities we can think of, and the more solutions we can find to correct problems.

Whenever we are able to lower our brain frequency, our

awareness improves, as does our hearing. Once I was invited to a house to work with a person who had a headache. The TV was on and I asked for the volume to be lowered. The person put the TV on mute and no sound was heard. However, when I reached a relaxed mental state to begin the healing work, I could hear every word on the TV even though it was still on mute.

Try this experiment for yourself. Sit quietly, with your eyes closed and think about something pleasant for a few moments. Then just become aware of the sounds you hear that you hadn't noticed before. The information isn't new; it has been around for a long time.

One of my teachers, Tom Brown, who was trained by an old Apache medicine man by the name of Stalking Wolf, was given similar information around 1962. Stalking Wolf didn't call them frequencies, he called them lands. Alpha was the "land of the Spirit," theta and delta were "lands of the shaman" and beta was the "land of the living dead."

In the shaman training with Tom Brown, I learned how to walk in such a manner as to stay in alpha for indefinite periods of time. It is a level of mind that allows us to be aware of things around us and also those at a distance, and also to be able to receive information not available at the beta level.

I do not hear rap music. Why? Because I do not tune my radio to the frequency where it exists; therefore, I do not hear it. Information from the spirit world does not seem to exist in the beta frequencies. We need to reach a lower frequency to tune into this type of information.

Achieving Alpha

Now this is enough technical stuff. Let's get into how to do it. There are a lot of methods to achieve the same purpose. Most are presented in a far more complicated way than is necessary.

Alpha is not some mysterious realm off in another faraway land. It is simply a frequency reached by lowering the brain waves. We do this by relaxing the body and mind.

How do we relax the body? By doing something we have been doing all our lives. It's called breathing. What do you do when you are stressed out and something else happens to add to the stress? You probably take a long breath and let out a sigh. Most of us do. It is a natural way of reducing stress. We don't even have to think about it, we just do it.

If you were here with me, I would ask you to close your eyes while I take my drum, and with a rapid beat would ask you to take a deep breath and build it up and up and hold it, and then let it go. This is a very deep breath and is released with force. Then you would take a deep and gentle breath and imagine yourself at the beach. Feel the cool water on your feet, the sun on your skin, hear the sound of the waves, smell the water, and feel the difference in the temperature of the water and the rays of the sun. Then you would take a deep breath, and while inhaling, pretend to write in the sand. You could write your name three times, or you could write whatever you like. Then, as you exhale, pretend to have a wave come in and wash out what you have written. Take another deep breath and pretend to write the same thing again two times. Again exhale and pretend to have the wave wash out what you have written. Take another deep breath and pretend to write the same thing again one time. Again exhale and pretend to have a wave wash it out.

By taking a deep breath and bringing back the memories of being at the beach and writing and erasing, you are forced to use the right side of your brain. Also, by thinking of something pleasant, you are relaxing your mind. You don't have to use this method. Any method of deep breathing and thinking of something pleasant and using the five senses will work for you. Later on we will discuss how to reach the same level of relaxation by walking a path with flowers and trees. Now isn't that simple?

Many people have asked how you know when you are at the alpha level. Good question. No bells will ring, no horns will blow, and there will be no formal announcements made. Just assume that you are there. If you are like a little kid going on a trip who keeps asking, "Are we there yet?"—you aren't.

After a few sessions, you will feel the relaxation and become familiar with the feeling. If this helps any, how many times have you driven some distance not remembering the last few blocks or miles? You were daydreaming, and that takes place at the alpha level. As stated earlier, alpha is not some mysterious realm off in another land, just a state of relaxed body and mind. Don't complicate it!

Programming

Once you are there, what do you do about it? Program yourself. What does program mean? To program yourself means to plant a suggestion in your mind that will cause you to react in a desired manner in the future. Let's take some real-life examples. I have programmed myself to "be aware of any and all danger to myself, family, and friends, and to take the appropriate action to avoid the danger."

One morning I was awakened by a dream that seemed significant. After getting up, I used my pendulum to get answers to a few questions like: Does this apply to me? Does it apply to any of my friends? Which one? I was able to determine that an ambush was being set up for one of my friends. By changing the energy of the situation, we were able to avoid the planned ambush.

Now you may ask, "How do you know it would have happened?" All I'm comfortable with putting into print is that in the following twenty-four hours there was sufficient evidence to indicate such a plan had been in place.

So you ask, "What is a pendulum?" It is a weighted object on a string or chain. It can be something elaborate like a semi-precious stone on a silver chain or as simple as a nut on a string. Dowsing will be discussed in chapter 7 and a chart is located at the end of the book.

Scrambling Frequencies

Another time—one evening—I got the message that a friend was in danger, and I tuned in to him to see what was happening. He didn't answer his phone so I just left a message to call me when he got in. I got the impression of his tractor turning over, and I changed the energy of the accident. Later, when he called, he confirmed that he had been in a dangerous situation with the tractor. The tractor had been about to turn over with him. One wheel had already risen from the ground, but it seemed that something had set the wheel back on the ground. Was it the power of my thoughts?

I have a friend who works as an undercover cop. One day he came to mind, and upon checking into his situation, I discovered a plan to kill him. Again, the energy of the planned attack was changed and a few days later he came by to visit. When I asked if he had upset anyone's plans, he confirmed that he had been involved in a drug raid and that there had been threats on his life.

Recently, I knew my friend Larry was driving from Montreal to Toronto. Just before dark, I got a flash or picture of his car crashing into a truck. Using my dowsing system, I scrambled the frequency of the accident and created a mental picture of his car passing the truck unharmed.

The next day when he called, I asked, "Just before dark last night did you almost collide with a truck?"

He replied that a truck had stopped right in front of him and he was able to swerve around it, but he didn't know how.

How did all this happen? Simply by planting an idea in the mind "to be aware of all danger to myself, family, and friends and to take the appropriate action to avoid the danger." Ok, so you want to know what a dowsing system is and how I neutralized the ambush. Keep reading, it will be explained later.

There ought to be a way to write all these things with information flowing smoothly from one idea to another, but I haven't found it yet. So with that in mind, expect to read some statements that don't seem to fit in anywhere. This is a book to help you improve your life, not win some literary award.

There is a lot more we can do. We can plant suggestions to be at the right place at the right time, to attract to us the people we need for whatever purpose, to be kind to our family and friends, to overcome fear and/or anger, to work efficiently and cheerfully. We can plant suggestions to achieve most anything that would improve our lives. The important thing is to be sure that you plant the correct idea in your mind. What I mean by this is, your subconscious mind will not take a joke. It seems to take everything literally.

Just this week I learned how true this is. Rick, my mechanic, is always there when needed to keep my vehicles going. I wanted his business to succeed so he would continue to be available. Every time, after buying an old truck, I would always say to him, "Looks like I'll be keeping you in business." I have, beyond my wildest dreams! The trucks keep breaking down.

Listen to yourself *talk!* Listen to yourself *think!* Realize what you're doing to yourself!

My friend Karen lives over 600 miles away. When her hip was hurting, she would call me to take the pain away. In an effort to save her a phone call, I programmed myself to be aware of any time she had any pain in her body. I also gave myself the suggestion that I would be able to remove the pain. So far it has worked. At various times I would get a mental message that she was hurting. I would then imagine her standing in front of me and me moving my hands around her in the same manner as if she were physically present. That evening after she got home from work, I would call and say something like this: "Your hip was hurting at 3 P.M. today." Her reply would be something like this: "Yes, but I felt you come and fix it."

Let me say here that this does not work for everyone. It seems that there has to be some type of connection to the person, but I really don't know what it is. Neither is this to be taken by readers that people can write to me asking for the same thing. The idea is for you to learn to do it.

Remember that the most important message I have for you is that you have a *choice.* Now you are beginning to see how to make some choices and to gain some control of your life. But there is more.

The Power of Thought

All things are composed of energy, in one form or another, even our thoughts. Brain frequencies can be measured by machine because they are electrical impulses—so they must be composed of electrical energy.

Several years ago, while laying brick on a construction job at a college, I looked in the window of the science building and noticed a chart of atomic weights. Hydrogen had one proton and one electron; gold had 80 protons and 80 electrons. It seemed that the difference between hydrogen and gold was simply the number of protons and electrons composing the atom of the element.

In school we had learned that protons and electrons were charges of electricity. And what is it that our brains emit continually? Charges of electricity. Therefore, it would appear that thoughts are things. Thoughts are composed of the same energy that makes up everything around us. If this is true, then we ought to be able to create future events with our thoughts. It seems that we can.

A few pages back, you read about reaching a relaxed state of mind by writing in the sand at the beach. In class, the folks are led through this exercise. I have them imagine, or visualize, floating in the ocean and each time a wave washes over them, it carries away the pain from their body. Most of those who experienced pain before the exercise find that the pain is much less, or nonexistent, afterward.

Another method I use in class to achieve the same degree of relaxation is a drumbeat. This gets a bit more advanced, because the folks attending my classes also learn how to send healing energy to other people. I make no claims to be a drummer but it seems to work anyway.

While listening to the drum, they imagine walking a path, feeling the Earth under their bare feet. They will imagine reaching out and feeling the bark of trees, smelling and touching the flowers, and employing all of their five senses. This causes them to use both the right and left sides of the brain and they reach a very relaxed state. While they are relaxed, I will slowly repeat beneficial statements to them and allow them time to mentally repeat beneficial statements of their choice. One of the statements is: "I am always aware of any and all danger to myself, family, and my friends. I take the appropriate action to prevent or avoid the danger." Other statements that are repeated include the ability to be at the right place at the right time and to be able to reject any nonbeneficial subconscious messages.

Listening to these statements while in this relaxed condition causes the brain to absorb the information and respond when needed. Please be aware that the brain will absorb and act upon *negative* messages also. In the appendix you will read how

Dick Sutphen describes this in detail. It is very important that we listen to ourselves talk and listen to ourselves think. Do not speak or think anything unless you want it to happen!

Brain Waves and Dowsing

My friend Ed Stillman from Sedona, Arizona, has done some extensive brain wave research in connection with Harold McCoy at the Ozark Research Institute (ORI). For six years, Ed was the scientific advisor for the American Society of Dowsers (ASD), where he was in charge of a research project on the brain wave responses of dowsers while the people were actually dowsing.

Ed has published two articles in the *ASD Journal* on the results of these dowsers' brain wave responses. He is currently the scientific advisor of the Ozark Research Institute, where he has been working on the brain wave responses of healers during distant healing. He is also president of the ASD Verde Valley chapter in Arizona. He is an excellent water dowser and won the national "Dowser of the Year" award for the U.S. in '99. He was looking for a place to drill a water well in northern Arizona and with his dowsing rods, he found it. The drilling rig was set up in the designated spot and drilled for 1,900 feet in the Arizona high country Ponderosa pines. A very good stream of water was found right where he said it was. There is a picture of this hanging on the wall of Ed's house, him standing there with an overflowing bucket of water. He looks quite happy with the results, and no wonder, finding water at 1,900 feet!

The following information on brain wave research was written with quite a bit of assistance from Ed, who is much more of a scientific writer than I. I am stating this in case the reader is wondering why this writing doesn't match the rest of the book.

Dr. Matthew Kelly of Sedona, Arizona, has measured and analyzed the brain waves of both dowsers and remote healers. Dr. Kelly measured the brain wave frequencies of Harold McCoy as a test subject. Dr. Kelly made the brain wave measurements and Ed wrote an article on Harold's brain waves. The testing used a standard protocol, identifying each part of the process and taking the test measurements. This article appeared in the *ORI Journal* and Ed presented the results of this study at the ORI conference in April 2002. Here is a brief summary of his findings:

Dr. Kelly used medically approved brain wave measurement and analysis equipment to map the brain waves of Harold McCoy, a highly experienced distant healer. His findings showed that all four of the primary brain wave frequency bands were active in a highly coherent pattern whenever Harold reached his "healing" state of mind. This helps verify that our minds are most effective when we can reach a relaxed state of mind that is both deeply meditative in the alpha brain wave state, and yet actively aware in the beta state, with high conscious awareness and focused attention.

There is more to the findings. During the distant-healing, brain wave-measurement session, unusual amounts of both the subconscious theta and unconscious delta frequencies were highly active in Harold's brain waves at the same time the coherent beta and alpha frequencies were measured. Coherent means that the neurons in Harold's brain were firing in synchrony in diverse areas of his brain. His brain was operating at a high power level and was completely engaged in his distant healing task during those parts of the testing.

The theta frequencies are thought to provide intuitive input, and delta frequencies are thought to be the frequencies that provide our deepest psychic awareness. Harold believes that delta frequencies constitute a key part of distant healing by becoming the transmission frequency range to the remote subject. Perhaps this is why delta is referred to as the "land of the shaman."

The Power of Suggestion

Now that we know a bit about brain frequency, let's take a look at a more elaborate piece of information.

The fierce loyalty of people to certain organizations puzzled me. For example, in the Army, we were brainwashed to support our higher-ranking people, not because they were necessarily any better or smarter than the rest of us, but because they had a different emblem on their collar. In religion, people will defend their priest or minister regardless of what they may have done. In mind development classes, which I have both taken and taught, it was noticed that students were ready to burn incense to the instructors and leaders. This just didn't make any sense and for years I wondered, "Why?"

Then my friend Mike Kalka sent me a tape of "Battle for Your Mind" by Dick Sutphen, who is a very well-known author and public speaker in the metaphysical world. His company, Valley of the Sun Publishing, markets his subliminal tapes and he is a recognized authority on this subject. In the tape, Dick explains why people respond to suggestions when they are not even aware they are doing it. It answered a lot of questions for me. I copied the tape and passed it on to friends, because Dick had given permission to do so in the tape. He was generous enough to allow me to reprint the text in this book, which is located in the appendix. Being aware of a problem is the first step in eliminating it. When you read Dick's words, see if any of them apply to you, because many of us have been brainwashed and didn't know it.

By implanting positive suggestions in our minds, perhaps we can prevent someone from influencing us in a negative manner. Here is an idea you might want to use. Put your mind and body in a relaxed position and mentally repeat, "I am always aware of all attempts to adversely manipulate my mind. My mind always rejects any suggestions that are non-beneficial to me."

You can also do this for your kids. Write a list of positive statements about them, such as "you are kind, you are neat, you are intelligent, you are loving, you like vegetables," and the list goes on. If your child is young enough that you still put them to bed at night, you can repeat the statements as soon as they close their eyes. You can also repeat the statements before you wake them in the morning. I suggest that you use the child's name and repeat the positive statements several times. Remember, keep the statements *positive!* Avoid using words like *not* and *don't.* Think about it a moment. If someone told you not to think of a pink elephant, you already have.

If your children make a mistake, don't tell them they're stupid. Tell them that they are much too intelligent to do what they just did. If they make a bad decision, tell them they are smarter than that. Tell them, "Someone as smart as you can make much better choices than the ones you made."

I have observed parents talking about their child to others, while the child is listening, and telling the listener what a brat the child is. Or, they talk directly to the child about how bad or mean they are. In every case, the statements have been true. The power of suggestion works negatively too. Whatever you do, tell them not to believe much of what they see on TV. I read a statement recently that the producers of TV shows for young people really don't influence the children, they *own* them!

Suggestions and My Daughter, April

Let me give some personal examples of how positive suggestions have worked for us.

The night my daughter, April, was born, I repeated to her a

number of times, "Every day in every way, April is getting better and better and better." I did this each night and morning. When she first started talking and putting words together, guess what she said?

When April was about a year and a half, we had a problem with airplanes flying too low over our house. Apparently we were on a flight path for military planes on training exercises. The planes would come over the mountain low and loud. April would be in the yard and would come running to the house crying. After a couple of times, I figured it was time to do something about it. I asked her if she liked the airplanes?

"No!"

"Do you want to chase them away?"

"Yes!"

"OK, next time you see an airplane coming over the house, stay where you are. There is no need to be afraid of it, just point your finger at it and it will go away."

Next day, she was out in the yard and the plane came over the mountain. She started to run for the house.

"Stop!" I told her. "Point your finger at it and it will go away."

Up went her finger, pointing toward the plane. I encouraged her, "See, it's working. Keep pointing, it's leaving!"

I continued to encourage her to chase the plane away. Anytime after that, when she saw a plane approaching, she would point her finger at it and sure enough, it would fly away. They never frightened her again.

When April was about three years old, she got a kidney infection. Her doctor told me that she needed to drink more water. I tried to convince her to drink water, but she replied that she wasn't thirsty. That night when I put her to bed, I repeated very softly, "April is thirsty. April wants water to drink, yum, yum, yum. Thirsty, thirsty, thirsty."

The same thing was repeated the next morning before waking her. When she got up, she wanted a drink of water. She has drunk plenty of water ever since.

We were home schooling her and at about the age of seven or so, she had the idea that boys were better at math than girls. She really didn't like doing math. One night after she closed her eyes, I repeated softly, "April is smart. April likes math. Math is easy. Math is fun."

These simple positive statements were repeated several times, both at night and in the morning. The next day, math classes got a lot easier.

Here is an example of the type of math problems she would work on:

"How many sandwiches can you make with a truckload of peanut butter? What information do you need to solve the problem?"

She would ask, "How much does a truckload of peanut butter weigh?"

"One ton."

"How many pounds are there in a ton?"

"2,000."

"How much do you put on each sandwich?"

"One ounce."

It was simple math to find that 32,000 sandwiches could be made with a truckload of peanut butter. Then we would figure how many loaves of bread it would take.

Here are some more examples of her math problems:

"If you want to have a party and give each guest two cups of hot chocolate, how many people could you invite if you had a 55-gallon barrel of hot chocolate?"

"How many times would a rabbit have to hop from here to get his feet wet in the Atlantic Ocean?"

"How many burritos laid end to end does it take to reach across Texas?"

"How many cucumbers laid end to end does it take to stretch from here to the Georgia state line?"

All of these questions may seem complicated at first glance, but when the needed information was provided, they were quite simple. Solving problems like this gives a child a feeling of confidence in solving other problems. It causes them to think.

We always encouraged imagination and observation. Every time April, as a three-year-old or so, would stop to look at something, I would say, "You are very observant, this is good."

By being told she was observant, she became even more observant. One day when she was four, we went to the bank. While I was at the teller window, she was looking at a small tree in the lobby. She came to me and said, "Daddy, there is something strange about this tree. The wood is real but the leaves are artificial."

When I examined the tree, I found that the trunk of the tree was a piece of wood with holes drilled in it, and plastic leaves had been inserted into the holes. I have often wondered, of the thousands of people walking through that lobby, how many noticed this.

One day while my wife, Nancy, and April, at age three, were visiting a friend, April noticed that a small bush beside a basement window was moving, as if blown by the wind.

April said, "That bush is moving but the wind isn't blowing. We better check this out."

A quick look showed that the exhaust from a clothes dryer was vented beside the bush, making it move.

To improve her imagination, we would play games. One went something like this:

"April, you have one minute to look at me. Notice everything about me."

At the end of one minute, I would say, "Close your eyes. Now tell me, what color is my hair? How long is it? What color are my eyes? What color is my shirt? Does it have pockets? How many? Do the pockets have flaps? Do the flaps have buttons or snaps? What is on my head? What color is it? Now pretend my shirt is red. Pretend it is blue. Pretend there is a parrot sitting on my shoulder. Pretend my hat is green. Pretend a crow is sitting on my hat."

The number of things for her to pretend continued, and I made them ridiculous to keep her attention. I always use the word "pretend," when working with children. They understand it better than "imagine" or "visualize."

One day when April was seven, we were working with some other kids who had been coming to visit and learn survival techniques. I pointed out two trees, an oak and a poplar, and told them to pretend to walk into the trees and tell me which tree had the hardest wood. Everyone picked the oak tree and they were right. It is amazing what a child can do if they don't know they can't do it.

If you want your child to believe something, then incorporate it into the stories you tell them. Think about it, this is what television programs have been doing for years. You have to do it yourself, you can't depend on your babysitter or the teacher at school. It is your kid. It is your job.

Let me give one example of incorporating an idea into a story:

When we would go to town and stop at the health food store, April would want a soy milkshake. She wanted one in a soft bag-like container. Problem was, she squeezed it and then it would run down her arms and make a mess. I suggested that she get one in a box but her heart was set on the one in the bag. That night for a bedtime story, I told of a little girl who saddled her pony to ride on a trail with her pet fox and pet crow. We went through the details of saddling the pony and packing the saddlebags with goodies for a picnic. There was dog food for the fox and corn for the crow and for her there was a banana, a sandwich, and a milkshake in a *box*. I described the trail and all the animals she saw as she rode her pony to a spot for a picnic. She fed the dog food to the fox; the corn to the crow; and she ate her sandwich, banana, and drank her milkshake from the *box*. The next time we went to the store, she wanted a milkshake in a *box*. Power of suggestion is a wonderful thing if used positively rather than negatively.

The same principle applies to many other things. Never let a day pass without telling your children that you are proud of them. Take every opportunity to compliment them and cause them to feel good about themselves. This doesn't mean that bad behavior should be tolerated. It should be corrected. That is one of our jobs as parents. It is my belief that a child will live up to, or down to, our expectations. If the people in positions of authority had received better training when they were children, the world would be in better shape now. If you have children, you can help them to make a better world for themselves.

2 Misfits

It is probably time for a story of how we can use our minds to influence future events. Once upon a time I gave some thought to how we might help some unfortunate souls improve their lives and families. Having little idea of how to go about this, a thought or intent was simply sent out to the universe. A couple of days later, I got a call from a local social service agency that wanted to offer a stress management class for their employees. Would I be interested in applying for the job? Yes, of course! I asked for the names of the hiring committee, but they weren't known at the time. The agreement was that I was to meet with the committee the following week. There were four positions to be filled and 12 applicants. No applicant would fill more than one position.

Now, this was an opportunity to be taken advantage of. That night just before going to sleep, I reached a relaxed mental and physical state with the method described earlier and gave myself the mental suggestion that I would wake up when the committee was most receptive for communication. Sometime during the night I woke up, at which time I imagined some blank faces and gave them the title of "the committee." Then I sent them the thought that "I will meet with you for evaluation and you will agree to hire me because of the value I have to offer." Next, I imagined myself teaching the class, getting paid, and taking the check to the bank.

When the meeting took place, it was taken for granted that the job was mine. Of the four positions to fill, I filled two of them.

This was the start of teaching for five counties in the state and being able to help a number of people who seemingly would have had no other way of getting the information to help themselves. The people in those classes were mostly single mothers on welfare, and at first were reluctant to be there. The first class was composed of those who had not responded to any other type of training.

Now, when I go to a place to hold a class, the room is usually filled with smiling faces, and some good person is always there to introduce me in terms that are so complimentary and sometimes overstated that it is an embarrassment. I look around to see who they are talking about. Not so with this class. We were simply put in a room together and the door was closed. Looking at the faces glaring back at me, the stories of Christians being thrown to the lions crossed my mind. Later I was told that the only reason they were there was because it was a qualification they had to meet to continue to get food stamps.

These women had experienced enough of men in suits standing behind a podium and talking over their heads. That is what they expected and that is what they were prepared for. They sat there, arms folded, teeth clinched, ears closed, and mouths shut, prepared to endure until I had finished and then they would get up and walk out. Well, I hadn't worn a suit because I didn't have one. Gave it away about 30 years ago. I just went over to where they were sitting around a table and sat down on the table in front of them and asked, "How many of you have kids?" All hands went up.

"How many of you are exactly where you want to be in life?" No hands went up.

"How many of you want your kids to wind up just like you?" No hands went up.

"OK, if I could show you some ways to help your kids so they don't grow up like you, would you be willing to listen?" Heads nodded.

On the third day of the class, some members of the agency came in to count the dead and notify the next of kin. Since there were none, I took the opportunity to open up another can of worms. Figuring it would either make or break me, I asked, "Would someone who has learned something please stand up and tell our visitors about it?"

One woman, who had sat there three days with her head down, stood up and said, "I stopped half the fighting in the house the first night after the class."

Another woman caused her daughter to stop bedwetting and the next day brought one of her neighbors to the class.

Now in all honesty, not everyone transformed their lives, but those who put some effort into it did. At the end of each class, I passed out paper and pens and asked them to write what they thought of the class, good, bad, and indifferent, and it was not necessary to sign the paper. No one ever handed in a negative paper and everyone signed it.

My friend Jack Kestner, who writes a weekly column for the *Bristol Herald Courier* newspaper, did a story on the results of the work based on the letters written by those attending the classes. No sooner were the papers printed than there was an outcry from someone in the religious community accusing me of "dangerous mind-altering techniques" and that "local residents were being seduced toward this New Age thinking." A few weeks later, Jack did an excellent rebuttal, making the woman who wrote the accusation look pretty silly. Jack is good at that.

I would like to take this opportunity to personally thank that woman for writing about these "dangerous, mind-altering techniques." It told me a lot about the way people think, or don't think, as the case may be. It is for reasons like this and the following, that Dick Sutphen's "Battle for Your Mind" is included in the appendix.

Challenges

As time went on, the opportunities to work with the people on welfare increased and the job was both challenging and rewarding. Challenging in that some of the people just refused to learn anything. I remember one woman who protested learning to relax. She was polite enough about it, just stated that she would not participate in any activities in the class because of her religious beliefs. I answered her by saying, "But all we are going to do is learn to relax."

She informed me in no uncertain terms that she got her relaxation from Jesus. My reply was, "If it's OK with Jesus, it's OK with me."

At break time I asked the director if he would permit her to leave and he agreed. The energy of the class was greatly improved after that. Reminds me of attending a mountain man rendezvous once where we sat around the fire at night and swapped stories. The next morning, the emcee announced, "Don't know which one of you it was, but when you left last night, things sure got a lot better."

Then there was the woman who refused to participate in the mental exercise that we use to develop a pain-control technique.

The exercise requires that we imagine putting our hand into a bucket of hot water to see if our hand will get warmer. Her reasoning, I'm sure, was based on previous experience, for she announced to the entire class, "If you put your hand in hot water, you will pee on the floor!"

They were an interesting group. One woman disrupted the class so much that the next time they were at any semblance of relaxation in an exercise, I planted the suggestion in her mind that she would leave the class. When the exercise was completed, she promptly got up and walked out, never to return.

How did I do this? Simple. I just reached a state of mental relaxation, which probably put me on the same frequency she was on, and created a mental picture of her walking out. She got the message on some level of her consciousness and responded.

Now there is usually one person in every class who is concerned about affecting the behavior of others. Most of these folks have good intentions and are harmless. Problem is, they aren't the type of people who do anything to improve conditions. Sometimes it seems that they just didn't like my way of doing things and took offense at my direct methods. In one instance, a woman verbally attacked me during a talk I was giving showing how to use these methods. With venom in her voice, she accused me of "interfering with another human being." I asked her, "How many children have you prevented from being abused or molested with your attitude? How many women have you prevented from being beaten or raped with your apathy? How many serial killers have you stopped with your non-involvement? Damn right, I interfere with other people who are abusing innocent and helpless ones."

It was another one of those cases where things got a lot better after she left.

Back to the welfare ladies. One who sticks in my mind was the woman whose manner of dress, or lack thereof, revealed some remarkable tattoos. There was little doubt in my mind that she held a position of esteem in the local chapter of Hell's Angels. As I said, they were an interesting group.

Once, on the first day of class, a woman approached me with the request; "Will you help my son stop wetting the bed?"

"No," I replied, "you will."

"But I don't know how."

"You will." I answered.

I explained to her that she must reach a relaxed state of mind after her son was asleep and send him a mental message that he would "get up, go to the bathroom, take care of his need, get back in bed, and go to sleep. In the morning your bed will be dry." It was explained that she needed to visualize this taking place because the brain thinks in pictures rather than words. I often ask my class, "How many of you would like to speak a universal language?" All hands go up.

Then I say, "You already can. It's pictures."

The next morning she was so excited because her son had gotten up and gone to the bathroom and the bed was dry. But she had a complaint. He wouldn't go back to sleep.

"Did you tell him to go back to sleep?"

"No."

"Then tell him tonight."

That night he got up, went to the bathroom, and got back in bed and went to sleep like he was supposed to. When sending messages like this, be sure to fill in all the gaps.

Once, while staying in someone's home with a seven-year-old boy, I observed that he had plastic pants put on him before bedtime. This seemed odd, so I asked, "Why?"

· "Because he has always wet the bed," was the answer.

That night I sent him a message, and the next morning the

boy's clothes were dry. The parents wanted to know why. That was about seven years ago, and just this week the word came that the boy had never wet the bed after that night.

Why It Works

Many times people ask me, "Why does this stuff work?"

It works because we *do something!* If we *do nothing*, then we can be assured that *nothing* will happen. If we do *something*, then *something* might happen.

My friend Don Yows, from Missouri, has a business card with his name, address, and these words: "Keep on doin' what you're doin' and you'll keep on gettin' what you're gettin'." It is human nature to resist change, but unless there is change, there will be no improvement.

Let's direct our attention back to the classes for the women on welfare. Some really excelled and got jobs and set goals for getting off welfare and improving their lives. One lady went to college and had enough influence to get me invited to speak nine times at that college. It was getting exciting!

Now you might be wondering if the results were so successful with these folks, why aren't I still teaching those classes? Well, there are a number of reasons, most of which will be denied by those in authority. I didn't look the part, dress the part, or act the part. Just didn't fit in with the system.

Oh yes, they were nice folks and I liked them and appreciated the opportunity to work with them, but faded jeans, boots, long hair and beard, not to mention a bear claw necklace, just doesn't cut it with the suit and tie crowd. It doesn't seem to matter about the results; it's the look that counts.

I'm reminded of a scene from a movie—believe it was *Easy Rider*. The star was riding a motorcycle through the deep South in the sixties and his looks didn't fit in with the locals, so he was thrown in jail with a lawyer who was there for being drunk. The fellow couldn't figure out what he had done to deserve such treatment. The lawyer told him something like this, "You stand for freedom and it scares the hell out of 'em."

One day after delivering an empowering speech to my class, I was called aside by a person in authority and admonished for telling the class too much. These were his words: "You will get them to where we can't control them."

Looking back, I should have realized that if we got the people off welfare and they became independent, then the bureaucracy wouldn't have a reason to exist. I am convinced the main goal of any bureaucracy is to preserve itself.

Being more hard-headed than smart, I pressed on. One day a group of ladies from another county came by to visit the class, as they were considering hiring me for their area. The timing couldn't have been worse. We were near the end of the class and they were an above-average group with lots of promise. I really liked them, so I continued. "All your life you have been told what to do and when to do it and what you can't do. Someone else has made your decisions for you and your kids. It is time you stood up for yourselves and become independent. Take what you have learned here and start now to take your life back. Stand up, look people straight in the eye, and be proud of yourself and don't back down. You now have enough information to control your life and make your own decisions. Now use it."

The visiting ladies looked at each other with horror in their eyes and walked out. That was the last class I ever taught for the agency. All future classes were canceled.

3 Healing Techniques

My first exposure to any form of healing took place in 1973 in Augusta, Georgia, in a class called The Silva Method of Mind Control. The things taught in this class were very strange to me, since I was a product of the Appalachian Mountains and a very conservative religious background. Actually, the teachings contradicted most everything I had been taught in church. But something inside of me kept saying, "This is true."

The church where I grew up believed that Jesus performed miracles, as did the apostles, but modern-day healing was impossible. Irrational reasoning was applied, such as, "If people could heal today, then we wouldn't need doctors or hospitals." End of discussion. The idea of Native American healing practices was unknown to them and would have been dismissed as "unchristian."

I recall when Rolling Thunder, one of my teachers, visited us, the word must have gotten out because one good lady of the church called and demanded to know, "What does he believe about the Bible?"

I said, "Just a minute and I'll ask him."

Rolling Thunder replied, "Well, I try not to do anything against it."

This same question has been asked of me so many times I've lost count. Why is it when the subject of healing or using our minds and abilities to help someone comes up, there is some religious person trying to shoot us down? It seems that people fear what they don't understand and rather than trying to understand it, they attack it. Condemnation without investigation is the height of ignorance.

This seems to be the same mentality so abundantly used against the Native people of this land for 400 years. After all, if the church couldn't convert them to their brand of religion— put the fear of hellfire and damnation in them so they could control them—they might as well kill them. Those who do not conform to religion and the establishment are fairly useless to these agencies.

This reminds me of a story told by an Indian fellow in Northern Canada who had never before told his story to anyone.

He and other boys were sent to the residential schools when they were young. These schools were operated by the church but connected with the government. I am not aware of all the particulars but it seems the families didn't get any money from the government if the children weren't sent to the church-controlled schools. The children were forbidden to speak their native language and were made ashamed of their culture. They were beaten for the slightest reason or for no reason known to them. This man was in his mid-forties and he cried as he told me of the things he and the other boys suffered at the hands of those pretending to be representatives of God.

One rule was that no hair lotion was allowed. On a rare holiday when the boys were allowed to go home, some returned with bear grease on their hair. Now, the black robes would not tolerate such sinful practices in the house of the Lord and had a way to deal with it. There was a large industrial-size sink for washing mops and such. It was ideal for holding a young Indian boy's head under scalding hot water to wash out the demons in the bear grease. Never mind the screams, they were just sounds of repentance.

As this was being written, I received a call from a client in the Midwest. I related to her the story you have just read. She was quiet for a few moments and said with a sad voice, "This sure brings up a lot of memories of when I attended a religious school."

When she would ask a question in religion class, the question wasn't answered, but she was ordered to write some religious statement 500 times. Repetition is a convenient form of brainwashing. Those who ask questions the controllers can't answer are singled out as an example for discipline. That'll teach the rest of 'em to keep their mouths shut and do as they're told.

Misdirected Energy

In case you wonder why I'm telling these stories, it's because these problems don't go away just because they are ignored. There are oppressive people in this world because most people don't know anything can be done about it. Many of these people hide in pulpits, robes, uniforms, and public offices. In my next book, *Heroes & Friends*, I intend to tell a few stories of those who fought back. And won!

Please engrave this in stone. If you learn to use your mind and apply some of the examples in this book, you will be able to kick many of the oppressors in the seat of the pants. (I really wanted to say kick 'em in the ass but didn't want to offend you.)

The good folks I have been associated with religiously never did anything resembling the things just mentioned. They had good intentions but just didn't think things through very well. They listened to the preacher and took most every word to heart. If the sermons had been more positive, this would have been a good thing. It was abundantly quoted about God creating the Earth, but not once was there any mention of how we might use the power of prayer to heal the Earth or remove the pollutants from the water. The focus was put in the direction of fire and brimstone. I viewed all of this as a terrible misdirection of good energy.

But the church would pray for the sick, so I asked what the difference was in the apostles praying for the sick and us praying for them. If the apostles could do healing and we couldn't, why pray for them, since it wouldn't work anyway? It was explained that we would pray that the medicine prescribed by the doctors would help make them well. My reasoning was that if the medicine would do the job, then there was no reason to pray for them.

Looking back, I think they were partially right. It was in their belief system that the drugs prescribed by the doctor would help them. It was also believed that the prayers would help, too. Seems like they believed in the doctor more than the prayers, and if that is what they believed, they were probably right. A belief system is a powerful force—it defies logic.

Certain forms of healing were accepted, such as the use of herbs gathered in the mountains and made into medicine. As for the mountain folk who could stop severe bleeding or cause warts to disappear or take the fire out of burns—well, that didn't count.

When we are young, our minds have a tendency to absorb information without much questioning. And if we hear something enough times, we tend to believe it. Having attended church regularly for most of my life and hearing these things repeated, I had believed them. So when I learned of a technique to remove pain from the body, it was against all my religious teachings.

First Healings

But there is a saying, "The mind is like a parachute; both work better when open." In view of the previous explanations given by our ministers, I had the open mind. This pain-removal information excited me so much that I went in search of a victim. Next morning on the construction job, the superintendent had a headache and asked me for something to take it away, thinking I would offer him a painkiller.

"Stand still," I said. I put my hand close to his head and mentally employed the pain-relieving method learned the night before. All I did was mentally tell the pain to leave. His eyes got big and he started backing away.

"What happened?" I asked.

"Don't hurt no more," was the reply.

He didn't know it, but it scared me more than him.

How did this happen? I have wondered about it myself. Was I brainwashed into believing I could take away pain by just telling it to leave? Did I get him in a state of confusion where his subconscious mind accepted my mental suggestion and his body responded? Had I generated energy in my hand to overcome the pain? It has worked thousands of times since whether I understand it or not. The good thing about most of this stuff is you don't have to be smart to use it. *Just do it!!*

After that, the word spread and construction workers asked me to work on their minor injuries. Then after a while, they would take me home with them to work on their families. Maybe it was beginner's luck, but I had a high success rate. It was rewarding to be able to remove pain from old people who had suffered for years. There was so much I didn't understand about this, but wanted to share it with the world. Problem was, the world didn't want me to share with it.

At the next church service I made the announcement, "Jesus never cornered the market on healing and never claimed he did. We can do it too." Being reasonably kind people, they didn't make the motion to stone me to death, but they didn't believe me either. Why should they? After all, they had heard the same thing I had for most of their lives. The difference was, they never questioned it.

There was one elderly lady in the congregation who had caught her finger in an old-fashioned, wringer type washing machine. It was painful and crooked. She came up and asked if I could help her. I had always liked her and wanted so much to be of help. Taking her finger in my hand for a few minutes and visualizing her being able to straighten the finger, I said, "Now try and straighten it." She was able to straighten the finger with no pain and was most grateful. The rest of the congregation stood way back and were quiet.

I learned something about people that day. If you don't believe something, yet you can't deny its existence, then do the next best thing and ignore it and pretend it never happened.

One of the simple forms of healing used in my early years was simply to place my hand over the afflicted area and mentally tell the pain to leave, while symbolically visualizing the correction being made. One example of this was my granddad, who had poor circulation, and his lower legs and feet would get cold. As I passed my hand down his leg, a warm feeling could be felt until my hand reached his knees, then it became cold. In my mind, I visualized a river with logs floating down the river and a logjam was located at his knee. I imagined throwing a stick of dynamite into the logjam and breaking it loose. He remarked that he felt something jump in his knees, then his feet began to get warm.

Another time there was a man with a bandage on his ankle, who walked with a cane and limped. He described the pain as a coal of fire lying on the bone. I simply passed my hand over the ankle visualizing a coal of fire with water being poured on it and seeing the coal turn from red to black with steam rising from it. He looked at me and said, "The fire went out."

Three days later when we met, there was no bandage or cane and the pain was gone.

I asked, "How long had the pain been bothering you?"

"Fifteen years," he answered.

Healing at a Distance

Here is a story of healing at a distance written by Suzanne Cole of Sedona, Arizona. Suzanne and I met at the Southwest Dowsing Conference in Flagstaff, Arizona, in October 2000. We started talking and she told me of experiencing back pain and I offered to try and help her. The efforts were successful and she continued to keep in contact with me by e-mail. A friendship developed and she offered to help proofread this book and correct my spelling, which was quite a job. Here is her story as she has written it:

> Raymon saved me from ankle surgery for the removal of four bone fragments, much to my deep gratitude. I am a polio survivor in my early sixties and have had loose bone fragments, which had broken off within my ankle joint for years due to orthopedic surgery in the early '50s. In many past instances of pain caused by the fragments becoming jammed, I had manipulated my foot by hand and dislodged them, releasing the pain. Not so this particular time! I was in agony and could barely walk, so reluctantly went to my podiatrist. I told Raymon that the doctor wanted to schedule surgery right away. Suddenly the pain disappeared and the interior of my ankle joint felt smooth instead of gritty. I firmly believe that

Raymon's efforts permanently solved the problem, even though he was in Virginia and I was in Arizona. Healing energy knows no bounds of time or distance. This I know firsthand!

A year later, Suzanne's doctor was in the audience where I was speaking. I think she was joking when she said, "You're taking my business away from me."

My reply was, "No, I'm helping you be a more efficient healer."

Here is another example of healing at a distance. This letter was received when the person learned of this book being written and volunteered a story for it. The healing took place about three years ago. It is in the writer's own words.

> My husband had a very large gallstone. It bothered him off and on for years, then got so bad that he could not sleep at night and had trouble eating. I called Raymon and asked for his help. He said, "Well let's just look and see what we can do." I put my hand on Trav's shoulder and Raymon began working. I was in the middle, one hand on the phone and one on Trav's shoulder. The energy that came through me was overwhelming. Trav has not had any pain or discomfort since. He is always telling everyone he meets how cousin Raymon cured his gallstone.

This healing took place over a distance of about 3,000 miles. Distance is not a factor in transferring healing energy. I simply used the woman's body as a conduit for my intent to flow through to her husband.

Jeannie's Healings

My friend Jeannie, mentioned later in this book, has become a wonderful healer. She is especially good at feeling energy with her hands. Last year, while tearing down an old building, I fell and a large rusty nail stuck through my hand. Blood was squirting all over the place and pain was shooting all the way to my shoulder. I could tell that some nerves were damaged. I was able to stop the bleeding but the nerve damage was still evident. I called Jeannie and asked for some help. In about half an hour, the pain was gone and except for a hole in my hand, the hand and arm were back to normal.

Later, Jeannie told me that she had mentally put me on her healing table, could feel where the damage was, and worked at sending healing energy to the nerves. This was pretty good work for a distance of 300 miles.

Since this book is to encourage you to do something on your own, I asked her to write a few words about some of her work. Here they are:

My life has changed a lot since I took my first class from Raymon and learned that our minds are our most powerful tools. Raymon has asked me to share some of the things I have learned since taking his classes and to tell a story or two. The most important thing I have learned from Raymon is to have the courage and self-confidence to go ahead and try things that are out of the ordinary.

Once I learned to set my doubts aside and be open to new experiences, all kinds of interesting things began to happen in my life. Using dowsing to communicate with the spirit world and the universal field of information has opened a whole new realm of possibilities for me. After learning the effectiveness of dowsing and hands-on healing from Raymon, I went on to complete the Healing Touch certification program. I learned techniques that balance and unblock the energy field to relieve stress, reduce pain, and accelerate healing. In Healing Touch classes, we learned to gather information with a pendulum and to heed our intuition in a variety of other ways. Through my Healing Touch practice, I gained the skill of hand scanning.

Although I rarely see the human aura, my hands can detect the places in a person's energy field where there is a problem. This useful ability has made me very aware of the reality of the human energy field!

Although people respond to energy work in a variety of ways, I have found one fact that seems to hold true nearly all the time. In cases of injury, surgery, or sudden illness, the sooner you begin the energy work, the better the results. My husband has had severe kidney stone trouble in the distant past. This is a painful condition that can take hours or days to resolve, and often requires pain medication. In the last three years, my husband has had two kidney stone episodes. Each time, I was able to locate the problem area immediately with hand-scanning, and used techniques to clear and drain the energy blockage so his body could do its own healing more quickly. Both times, his severe pain subsided rapidly, and the episodes resolved in a day or two with minimum discomfort and no pain medication at all. Does this mean we shouldn't try to help someone who has a long-standing or chronic health problem? No, it just means we may need to try several sessions, and improvement may be gradual instead of dramatic.

Sometimes a long-standing pain will respond well to energy work, especially if it is related to an earlier surgery or accident. I worked at a distance with a friend who had pain from surgery a year earlier and swelling in the arm from lymph edema. There are as many ways to do distance healing as there are healers. My technique for this friend was to imagine her lying on my healing table. I used my hand-scanning and energy-balancing techniques as though she were really there. Although I know the actual motions are not totally necessary, for me it is helpful in focusing my intention. The friend reported the next day that her pain from surgery was gone. After subsequent sessions, she experienced a reduction of swelling in the arm. It appears that our energy fields can indeed interact with each other, both in person and at a distance. Thank you, Raymon, for teaching me the power of thought, and giving me the tools and the courage to try to make a difference. The results have been amazing.

A Third-Party Healing

Here is another example of using a third person for healing: My friends Larry and Rachel and I were traveling together to a conference in Iowa, where I was also invited to speak at the Unity Church. We arrived in town that evening and checked into a motel room. As Larry and Rachel were sitting on the bed talking, I was sitting on the other bed thinking. Experience had taught me that when we had three people together, our energy was greatly increased. I was thinking of the most appropriate way to use the energy of the three people present.

Suddenly the idea came to me. Larry had been involved in an accident 14 years earlier and his back had been broken. He still suffered some discomfort from this and had quite a bit of stiffness in his back. He walked with great difficulty, as if he were wading deep water. Larry and I had met about five months earlier while I was in Ontario and we had become friends. I had wanted to help him, but he did not seem to respond to the physical work I did. However, the mental work and dowsing seemed to produce favorable results. This was not unusual, as many of my male friends do not seem to respond to my physical energy, but will respond to the energy of a female.

Once before, I had enlisted the help of a woman to help me work on Larry. She took the right side of his body and followed my instructions as I worked on the left side of his body. Her efforts produced more results than mine did. This indicated he would respond more to a woman's energy.

I asked Rachel to place her hands just below Larry's belt and told her that the energy from her hands would go through his body to his back. She held her hands in this position while I was concentrating on the end result of improving his spine. Larry was lying on his back with his eyes closed during this time. After a few minutes, I took her hands and placed them on his hips, asking her to hold them in that position. No more than 10 minutes had passed when I said, "You can stop now. We've done all we can do."

Larry sat up and asked me to dowse with the pendulum to see if there were any steel plates in his back. After receiving a "no," I asked, "Are there supposed to be?" Larry replied that there had been steel plates put in his back 14 years ago after the accident. While lying on the bed, he had seen them disappear.

He said, "I can always feel them when I lie down and can feel the two screws that fasten them to my back." He then reached his hand around and felt his back. He had a strange look on his face as he exclaimed, "They're gone!"

The next morning he noticed that his back was much more flexible than ever before. After going back home, it was discovered that a metal detector would not be activated when held close to his back as it always had before. We thought this was interesting!

Not all healings are accomplished this quickly or easily, which is why we have to learn other ways of doing things. Sometimes all it takes is a thought or intent on our part to positively change the behavior of another. The trick here is to be able to focus that thought at the most powerful level of our mind. To be able to do this we must practice and train our mind. This is the reason the instructions were given in chapter 1. To be effective, we need to practice our healing methods while we have a relaxed mind. You can call it going to alpha, centering yourself, meditating, or any number of other phrases.

At this writing, a couple of years have passed. Larry went for an x-ray and the doctor told him, "Yes, there is something in there, but it doesn't look like steel. It looks more like bone."

Ah, but there is more. I had been thinking about time—I always get in over my head on this subject but think about it anyway. There are those who can write about time travel more eloquently than I, but please bear with me and allow me to try.

The Cave

One day Larry called to tell me about a strange experience he had had the day before. Seems like he had a spiritual visitor who had told him we needed to go to the cave.

"What cave?" he asked.

In non-verbal conversation, Larry was given the general location of the cave and the spiritual visitor disappeared. When he called to tell me his experience, I told him that I was aware of the cave, but didn't know the specific location. Tom Brown wrote of it in *The Vision*, in the chapter entitled "The Eternal Cave." This was a cave where it was possible to go into the future and the past. We were seriously considering going there as it seemed we were supposed to do. However, my friend Evelyn Rattray of British Columbia, who has a unique ability to converse with the spirit world, suggested I take Larry there in Spirit. Having quite a bit of confidence in Evelyn, I simply got Larry on the phone and said, "Get relaxed, we're going on a trip."

Being a good subject, he followed my directions and was able to mentally project to the cave. Once he was inside, I directed him to a passage leading into the past. Then I told him to find a hole in the wall, which would take him back to the time just before his truck had hit the tree. He replied that he could see exactly what had happened and it was very real. Almost yelling at him, I ordered. "Hit the brakes, stop the truck!"

A surge of energy went through his legs and he could feel an improvement. The next day he called to say that people were asking him what kind of treatment he had received because he was walking so much better. Since then, we have repeated this twice in a sweat lodge, each time getting better results. There is a fence between the sweat lodge and the yard. We have to swing our legs out and over it in order to cross the fence. The last time Larry came out of the sweat lodge, he was able to step across the fence in a forward manner by simply raising his foot and stepping across.

So, can we go back in time, make corrections, and have these corrections brought into the present? What are the limitations and what are the rules of the game? As with much of this stuff, there are a lot more questions than answers.

If you try this and get stuck 40 years back in time, send me a postcard.

Karen's Story

Now, this next story really belongs somewhere near the end of this book, but since I couldn't figure out where, I'll include it here. Karen, from British Columbia, is the friend mentioned in chapter 8. We got together again this summer. Here is her account of what happened.

> My name is Karen Embree and I am a student of shamanic healing. This is my story of learning and Larry's story of healing.
>
> In the summer of 1997 Bill and Winnie Askin invited me to their Northern Alberta homestead. That is when I first met Raymon Grace and Evelyn Rattray, a Tehltan native elder. Evelyn and Raymon conducted a healing for me that released me from the emotional memory of my body, mind, and soul, forever changing my life.

Over the next five years I became friends with these wonderful people and began training in shamanic healing. Among other things, I learned about power animals; soul retrieval; and releasing physical, mental, and spiritual blockages. A power animal is the animal that most closely reflects a person's inner strengths and personality. A power-animal journey is when a person goes into the spirit world and connects with their power animal. People often come back from these journeys with a better understanding of themselves. A person can return to the spirit world to learn from their power animals and receive guidance on daily life.

Soul retrieval is the practice of journeying into the spirit world to retrieve a part of a person's soul that has become separated. Soul pieces will shatter off and leave when a person experiences shock, trauma, or not being accepted. Sometimes a person will give away part of themselves or have it stolen. Soul loss is natural and protects a person during time of severe shock and trauma. When the shock or trauma is over and we are healing, the soul parts will typically come back on their own. Sometimes they do not come back and that is when we must go and find them, heal them, and bring them home.

In June of 2002, I traveled back to the homestead. The visit brought a challenge to reach into the deepest corners of the medicine bag to help one very special person. On a warm summer evening, Raymon introduced me to Larry Huszczo and life changed. This is where the story begins.

In October of 1986 Larry was the passenger in a pickup truck that had an unfortunate meeting with a tree. Larry was left with a broken back, a wheelchair, and a shattered future. By June of 2002, 16 years later, Larry was walking. Larry didn't walk the way most people do. He walked with high careful steps to swing his limp feet over the ground. The high steps created enough momentum so the feet would come down further ahead than where they had been lifted. He constantly scanned the ground for the safest, flattest place to set down each foot—a place that was free from the smallest of sticks and stones that were enough to throw him off balance and send him tumbling to the ground. There was little opportunity for Larry to catch his balance the way most people do; the muscles and nerves did not respond to adjust for weight differences. A loss of balance meant a trip to the ground or the floor if there was nothing to grab onto. He walked slowly, picked up one foot, carefully placed it down, shifted his weight, checked for balance, picked up the next foot, and repeated the procedure. It was slow, wobbly, exhausting.

Larry asked me to work with him, not really knowing what I did. Raymon and Larry had discussed some ideas and theories around soul retrieval. Both had believed that they had covered the bases for retrieving Larry's soul. We all had a lot to learn.

The night Larry and I started working together, the spirit guides took me to the site of the accident. A part of Larry was still at the accident scene. This part was still living the trauma, repeating the anguish and confusion over and over, like a broken record. Larry didn't really believe me, figuring that the trauma from the accident scene had already been healed, so we focused on the hospital. Larry told me his story of being confined to bed, hearing that he would never walk again. He talked about the wheelchair and the painful physical, mental, and emotional complications that went with the bed, the wheelchair, and the struggle to walk again. As he spoke, the story ran in full color in the spirit world. I saw the fragments of his soul, split from the whole, and hanging in their prisons of suspended animation.

The first night we determined there was a lot of work to do. The second night I journeyed to retrieve the soul parts in the spirit world and bring them home to Larry. The spirit guides took me to the accident site, hospital beds, wheelchair, crutches and canes, physiotherapy rooms, icy sidewalks, stairways, driveways, steps, and cold bare floors where Larry had experienced his trauma. That night the spirits healed anger, frustration, humiliation, embarrassment, hopelessness, fear, and an endless list of a complex range of negative emotions. They gathered Larry's self-esteem, inner strengths, hopes, dreams, joys, peace, compassion, balance, patience, and many more characteristics that had been lost. Each soul part told its own story—we heard why it had left, what needed to change so the soul parts would come back—and we called in the spirits again and again to heal the wounds.

As I journeyed to recover the soul parts, we did Larry's body-work, massaging the muscles and stimulating the energy flows with physical pressure, prayer, and vibration. The spirits brought a picture of a wooden finger trap where a finger goes in each end and both get stuck. This was to be visualized and placed in Larry's back. Each end would be filled with the severed nerves. They sent symbols to be drawn on his skin and songs of hope and healing to be hummed softly as my fingers traced the symbols over and over. They told me to draw lines from his back down each leg, over the muscles, and down to the toes. Larry felt the tingling sensation of the energy moving in his skin. Then they said to beat a hoop drum over his back and down the left leg. The drum vibration pulsed through his body, driving the energy first into the muscles, then deeper into the bones and the nerves. Wherever there was drumbeat, Larry felt a bolt of energy through that part of his leg. We worked on the left side, finding the soul parts, calling them back, gathering his power.

A sense of expectation hung in the air; it was time to see the results. Larry got to his feet and walked across the room, lopsided, stumbling, falling against the wall and the furniture. He looked so much worse than before and it was terrible to watch. Then he said quietly, "I can feel the carpet under my left foot but not under my right foot." He walked again, stumbling. I watched, carefully paying attention and realized that the left side of his body was moving totally differently than the right side.

Better? Worse? It looked good, but we were not sure. Larry lay down again and I drummed for the right side of his body. I prayed with every fiber of my being, inviting the spirits to do the same work for the right side of the body, fighting the fear that the magic of the first round would be lost in the second and Larry would have more hardship, not less.

He got up a second time and walked across the room. More balance, more control, more confidence, he could flex his feet more than ever. He smiled. "It has been 16 years since I could feel the fiber of the carpet through the bottom of my feet." He glowed. He went outside and walked barefoot across the rain soaked grass. Tears came to his eyes as he said, "I can feel the grass under my feet."

In the days that followed Larry integrated his soul parts by talking to them, hearing their stories, and calming their fears. He began remembering the emotions of the struggle, feeling the strength leaving him and staying with the chair, feeling the hopelessness as he fell again and again while learning to walk. Larry lived it one last time as he welcomed his soul home and felt his power return, waking daily to feel stronger, more alive, and focused. His balance had increased dramatically. We stayed in touch and he related how his friends and family were impressed by the improvement in his walking.

Four weeks later Larry invited me to visit him for several days and we began the next stage of his healing. Larry did a power animal journey to connect with his inner self. He was not only able to meet his power animal but was able to talk to him and receive guidance and advice. It was amazing to watch him as he explored the qualities of the power animal, calling on them repeatedly for help. The connection remains strong and grows continuously. The power animal's presence and personality is recognizable in Larry, and he has learned to tap hidden talents and has grown more comfortable in his own habits and personality.

Following the power animal journey, we continued with more soul retrieval work. We worked daily to bring home more soul parts that had been left behind, talking to them and bringing them into present time to participate in a fully mature conscious life. The retrievals were followed up with adjustments to belief systems and clearing of emotional memory and physical energy blocks. We brought back a part that had left at the age of three years. This part represented mischief and playfulness. The change was immediate and Larry began finding time to play and laugh just for fun. Larry reported this was a big change and he welcomed the depth and quality it added to his daily life.

One of the strengths of Larry's power animal is curiosity and it was valuable as we began exploring a different approach to healing. We wanted to understand more about how we were creating our own experience and use that knowledge to create an even better experience.

The future is raw, pure energy. A thought is an expectation of the future. When the thought meets the raw pure energy, it becomes reality. Reality may be as simple as a bookcase or as complex as a life-threatening illness. The spirit world does not judge good from bad, it simply provides what we ask for. When people use positive visualization, their future becomes filled with positive possibilities. These same people may also have hidden beliefs and subconscious expectations that are filling their futures with negative possibilities. All futures are filled with possibilities.

Larry and I developed a method for checking our future possibilities. When we discover a possibility that is negative or non-beneficial, we remove it, leaving only positive possibilities. Larry uses this check on a daily basis and five months after our first meeting, it provided a wealth of information on the impact of soul retrieval.

Larry came to see me about some hurdles that were not coming down. He was using his normally successful methods for managing attitude, energy, and healing but woke up one day with a very negative attitude and was very angry for no apparent reason. Larry checked his future that morning and many positive things he had worked hard to believe had vanished overnight, replaced with a future of negativity, destruction, and isolation. Something was wrong.

The spirit world directed my journey to the accident site and we recovered yet another part—Larry's core inner strength—was still at the crash. We retrieved him and he refused healing. The anger in this part was rejecting love, intimacy, gentleness, and patience and it had no desire to heal. Since this part was already affecting Larry's consciousness, we brought him back as a wounded part (normally we conduct the healing in the spirit world before the part is returned). This time the healing was done through a series of meditations to understand the wounds and release them. At the end of the day, Larry checked his future again; all had returned to the positive picture he had consciously chosen.

Larry says that his physical health has improved. His lower digestive system is stronger and functions with dependability and ease. His walking has improved and the most noticeable difference for Larry is the increase in balance. The most obvious difference for everyone else is that Larry does not lift his legs as high for normal walking and he walks with more confidence. Larry's feet barely moved when I met him and today he has both up-and-down and side-to-side flexing that can be measured in full inches beyond their previous ability. Larry also reported that he feels more relaxed about walking and does not watch so carefully. He has more of an intuitive sense of where the ground and other objects are. He says that happened when we turned on the radar in his toes and the results were immediate.

On a mental level, Larry says he is stronger, more focused, and has been able to connect with a new sense of purpose. He is more relaxed and accepting of daily life. Larry reports that his spirituality has increased, his faith is stronger, and he feels a sense of peace and contentment that was previously missing. Some of the most dramatic results have been on the emotional level where Larry feels optimistic and truly happy for the first time in his memory. He has been able to accept commitment, intimacy, and love where he had rejected it in the past and he is able to express his feelings and emotions, sharing love and gentleness with ease and comfort.

Every day we give thanks to the spirit world for the help. We give thanks to the spirit guides for the information and the healing. We give thanks for the teaching and the lessons brought forth so that we may learn and grow. Ho.

More Healings

Let's look at some other examples of healing situations. One of my friends owns a restaurant and her son works for her. She was telling me how he didn't smile enough; in her words, he was sour. She imagined pouring honey over him to sweeten him up. The next day he came to work whistling and smiling.

Another time someone who was working for me was very angry and depressed over the loss of a family member. I put him to digging a ditch and imagined that each time the pick hit the ground, he would release the anger and depression. By the time he finished, there was a remarkable difference in his attitude. All that was required was a mental picture of him working and a symbolic visualizing of the anger and depressions being released. By symbolic, I mean that I saw sparks of anger flying off him. This needed to be done while my brain waves were at a lower level to ensure the power of the thought. Another way of saying it, I created a mental picture and put *intent* into it. Also, there was a desire to help him and the emotion to help him. I believe that emotion is fuel for our intent.

Elise's Story

To give you some encouragement to *do something*, here is a letter from someone who *did something*.

Last year—March or April—you were here in Toronto for the Total Health Show. I came to the Toronto dowsers meeting and heard you speak for the first time. I had been using your techniques daily for about six months but had not had the privilege of knowing you.

A week prior to the meeting, I had a dream of a friend of mine in Vancouver, who at the time had chronic asthma (used his inhaler between six to twelve times per day). In the dream he was in the hospital dying and I saw this image of horribly weak and lifeless lungs. I didn't know what this meant and I felt helpless to help him.

After your presentation, I left feeling as though anything was possible and that there was absolutely no limitation as to who I was or what I was capable of accomplishing. That night I had another dream. This time my friend was healthy and vibrant and I saw an image of healthy, pink lungs full of life. When I woke from this dream I knew I had the ability to help him.

I called my friend and asked for permission to help him with his asthma using the techniques I had just learned from you. He agreed. I used your book, *Techniques That Work for Me,* and completed each page for my friend. Then I asked about his dependency and addiction to his inhaler and neutralized this. I dowsed to neutralize his food allergies to wheat, dairy, and chocolate; I checked the level of function of his lungs, which was low, and then raised this energy. I also checked the level of function of his kidneys, adrenals, liver, and a few other organs that all needed to be energized.

He called me a few days later to tell me how he was doing, although he had no idea what methods of healing I had used on him. He had stopped using his inhaler throughout the day and only had need of it first thing in the morning. He had more energy and had an easier time breathing. Two weeks later the status was the same, but he asked that I would dowse one more time.

I checked all the same things I had before. All was balanced except for his addiction to the chemicals in the inhaler. I scrambled the addiction and dependency to the inhaler and asked for self-esteem and confidence for my friend.

Raymon, for six months after the dowsing session, this man did not even own an inhaler—he could breathe with no effort and no amount of stress caused him to reach for the steroids. He eventually purchased a new inhaler but told me last week that he has literally used it three times.

Raymon, what you are teaching us is healing people and healing the world. You have given us the gift of believing in the moment—being free from bondage on all levels. I hope when you read this story you realize what an inspiring human being you are. When I listen to you speak I feel the pulse of freedom in my veins. Thanks to the Great One that I met you while my son is still young (four years old). He will now grow up knowing life without strings attached.

Thank you my friend, for *everything*.

Elise

Mike's story.

Mike Kalka and I have been friends for many years. He has done some amazing things with visualization and intent.

Back in 1993 when the storm of the century hit the East Coast, I was in a survival school with Tom Brown in New Jersey. The participants of the class were living in an old barn. We were bedded down in sleeping bags with some straw for a mattress. The door of the barn was about 12 feet wide and was never closed. Really, don't think there was a door, just a big opening in the wall for the wind to blow in. It was survival at its finest.

A subject of much discussion was whether the barn would withstand the wind that was forecast.

When the storm hit, some of the group waded out in knee-deep snow. About a hundred yards away from the barn, the wind was blowing so hard that it was necessary to bend over to prevent being blown down. There were several comments about the decreased velocity of the wind around the barn.

I wondered about this but didn't come up with an answer until speaking with Mike about a week later. Seems that he heard the weather forecast and knew I was in a barn somewhere in New Jersey. He put a mental shield around the barn to block the wind.

Now this is a bit strange; Mike was in South Carolina, the barn was somewhere in New Jersey. Mike did not have the location of the barn, but his intent worked anyway.

Another miracle that Mike did was to save a man's life by a very strange method. One day Mike got a call from someone whose friend was in the hospital and his brain was showing no response on the monitor. For all practical purposes, he was brain dead. The plan was to unplug him from life support in an hour.

Mike thought of a way to get the brain started again. He mentally put a spark plug into the brain that would spark with every beat of the man's heart.

At the appointed hour the life support was unplugged. But instead of gong to the morgue, the man walked out of the hospital.

Mike is a good fellow to have on your side.

Harold's Healings

As for going into the body to make corrections, Harold McCoy is a master of the trade. My friend Karen had suffered with fibromyalgia for years. We traveled together quite a bit, and this provided many opportunities to work with her. Getting the pain out of her hip was not a problem, but keeping it out was.

She and I were attending the Texas Dowsing Conference where Harold and I were speaking. In our conversation, I told Harold that my work with Karen had been very successful but really hadn't cured her. It seemed she needed energy from a person other than me.

Harold readily agreed to work with Karen, and to my knowledge, the problem was eliminated. It was not necessary for me to work with her any more concerning this. In speaking with him recently, I reminded him of his success and thanked him. He said he has had many successful treatments of fibromyalgia. He and the Ozark Research Institute have had many successful results with lots of people. What did he do? Seems like he just went inside her head and cleaned out whatever was causing it.

One of the most remarkable stories he shared with me was assisting a 43-year-old woman to become pregnant—through the use of non-physical means, I might add. All the normal "child producing" functions of her body had ceased. Harold just symbolically went inside the body and "cleaned up" all the reproductive organs. Over a year later he got a call from the woman, who then had a five-month-old son.

Sharon's Story

One of the more comical stories was the time my friend, Sharon, asked me to go with her to Florida to a meeting with lawyers concerning a car accident. She needed to collect enough money from the insurance company to pay her doctor bills. This was due to an auto accident where her car was hit by another vehicle while she was sitting at a traffic light. She wasn't trying to make any money, just get her bills paid. As we waited in the office, a lady came in who appeared to be very aggressive and asked for the key to the ladies' room. We guessed that this lady was the opposing lawyer who seemed to have the attitude of a grizzly bear with a sore tooth.

Thinking she would tear into Sharon, and that something needed to be done, I simply sent her a mental message that when she went to the restroom, she would drain out all her legal knowledge and aggressiveness. When she came back into the room, she glared at me with a look that said, "You're up to something. I just don't know what."

We went into the room with the long table and high-backed chairs. There were shelves of old law books that looked impressive but probably had never been read. I sat at the head of the table, smiling at everyone, especially the lady. In my mind I was creating a picture, telling her how beautiful she was, giving her a dozen roses and a box of candy, and then continued to flirt with her mentally. I had created a thought form of protection, like a big bubble, around Sharon to protect her from any hostilities. The lady lawyer got so confused that all she asked Sharon was her name and address. One would have thought the lady was representing Sharon. This stuff can be fun—and profitable. Sharon walked out with enough money to take care of the expenses resulting from the accident.

The Question of Free Will

OK, so the question comes up again, "Can I use this to take advantage of people?" or "You are interfering with someone's free will."

Well, I sure prevented the insurance company from taking advantage of Sharon. And yes, I supposed I interfered with the free will of their representative who was willing to let her pay her own doctor bills any way she could. Would I do it again? In a heartbeat!

Look at it like this. Do you pay your taxes willingly to support causes you don't believe in, or do you pay them to keep from being fined, having your possessions taken away, or going to jail? Is your free will being interfered with? Are you being taken advantage of? Are you being bombarded with subliminal messages every day that restrict your ability to make correct decisions? The society we live in is less than perfect. Using your mind just helps stack the deck in your favor.

4 Rolling Thunder

It would not be fair to write or talk about healing without mentioning some of my teachers. Rolling Thunder, for instance.

After practicing healing on all willing subjects for a few years, I was introduced to Rolling Thunder, who made a significant impression on me. It was one of those steps where life was never quite the same afterward. Here is the way it came about.

Reaching into the mailbox, I pulled out a copy of *The Mother Earth News*, and upon opening it, a picture seemed to jump off the page at me. That was in 1980 and it is still fresh in my mind. Walking back to the house, I read the story of a man who was saying things I had believed but had always been told were crazy, or at best, far out. I got to the house and told Nancy that here was a man I had looked for all my life and he would be coming to visit us.

She answered, "This man is famous. What makes you think he will come visit you?"

"Because I can feel it, and he will be here in October."

Three years later, in October, Rolling Thunder spent a week at my house.

Things have a way of working out. My friend Jack Kestner needed a cellar built and I laid the block for him at no charge. He, in return, enrolled me in a membership with The Association for Research and Enlightenment (A.R.E.) in Virginia Beach. The first batch of information from them included a seminar in which Rolling Thunder was a speaker.

Up to this point, we hadn't spent much money on seminars, but we decided to go. Things began to happen. The next week we met some nice folks who worked with the A.R.E. and had a large house with plenty of room. We were invited to stay with them and Nancy was given a free ticket because of her hearing loss.

Being eager to learn as much as possible, we got a front row seat in all the classes. The way I figured it, these speakers were smarter than I was and if I got close enough, some of it might rub off on me. I sat there with notebook and pen. At the end of three days, Nancy looked at my notebook and saw that it was blank. She asked, "What are they talking about?"

"Well, they are making some good talks, and are nice friendly folks, but I haven't learned anything I can use."

"If you don't know what they're talking about, let's go home," she suggested. (Nancy is real practical, like the time we went into a casino in Reno and she was watching people put money in a slot machine and pull the handle and then repeat the process over and over. She turned to me and asked, "Why do these people continue to put money into the machines when it is obvious they don't work?") After giving it some thought, I answered, "Let's stay and hear Rolling Thunder. Maybe he will say something I can understand."

After listening to Rolling Thunder and the drumming that night, something inside me woke up. It was like remembering something from long ago, but not being sure what. When he finished, I had seven pages of notes and knew what he had said. The next day there was an opportunity to meet him and it was one of those turning points in life. You know what I mean. Maybe you can't define it, but you can feel it and you know that life will never be the same again. I have been fortunate to have experienced several of these turning points.

A year and a half later, Rolling Thunder was in Richmond, Virginia, and again I was in the audience. He came back to me and shook hands and said, "Good to see you again." This blew my mind. He had seen thousands of people in the past year and a half. Why did he remember me? Not only that, he invited me to come visit him. I accepted and then invited him to come visit me and he accepted.

We didn't spend much time together and only talked on the phone now and then. Occasionally he would ask me to gather some herbs and send them to him. Even though our time was limited, there was something about him that I seemed to pick up but can't explain. One day we smelled his pipe in the living room and a few days later he called and made the passing remark, "I drop in to check on you from time to time."

One evening the two of us were out for a walk, and he said something that shocked me. "If you were to ask me anything, I would tell you, if I knew." This came as a complete surprise. There were thousands of things I wanted to ask him, but right then I couldn't think of a one of them.

My major objection to my teachers is that most of them have died before I learned enough from them. But then, I can't be them any more than someone can be me. We all have our job to do, and although we can benefit from the wisdom of others, we still have to do it ourselves.

Well, I had observed Rolling Thunder and had been given

some of his words of advice. Opportunities came that allowed me to try some of the things I had seen him do.

Lisa's Healing

Lisa was a 19-year-old waitress who was introduced to me by a mutual friend. She had irritable bowel syndrome and told me there was no cure for it. Not having any knowledge of the condition, I didn't know it couldn't be helped. This has happened so many times, we don't know something can't be done—so we do it. This is called intelligent ignorance.

I instructed her to come over just before sunset and to bring a piece of raw meat. This was completely strange to her but she followed the instructions. We went down by the creek where a fire had been prepared with cedar wood. The meat was placed on the ground beside the fire and Lisa stood nearby with a scared look on her face. This was understandable since none of this resembled a visit to the doctor's office.

Taking a feather, I symbolically cut her open, raked out the negative energy and shook it over the raw meat. When this was completed, the meat was put into the fire and burned.

On a hunch, I asked, "How long have you had this problem?"

"Two years," she answered.

"And how long have you lived where you do now?"

"Two years."

I asked her how she felt about where she lived and she answered that she felt closed in and afraid. There were a group of bikers in the upstairs apartment and she was afraid of them. Sometimes their music was so loud it shook her bed and she couldn't sleep. She stayed away as much as possible.

"OK, I need to come visit you one day," I told her. One day after work I stopped by, knocked on the door and one of her biker neighbors curtly told me, "She ain't home."

"That's OK, I'll wait."

Soon Lisa came driving in and I reached into my old truck and pulled out a burlap sack, threw it across my shoulder, and followed her into the apartment. From the sack I took an old bee smoker, which is a metal container with a billows used for producing large volumes of smoke. Beekeepers use it when taking honey from bees. I put cedar shavings into the smoker and set them on fire, then told her to wait outside and watch. In a few minutes, smoke was pouring out of the door and windows. Lisa was laughing nervously and it was attracting the attention of her biker neighbors. Walking outside, I drew a symbol on the door and reached into the sack, took something out, and rubbed it on the door. The motorcycles started up and in a moment Lisa and I had the place to ourselves.

A few days later she called to say the irritable bowel symptoms were gone and her apartment felt much better, just like home.

"And how are your neighbors?" I questioned.

"Oh, they moved out," she happily answered.

In all honesty, at the time, I didn't really understand what happened. Now, I understand a bit more of the situation. Since all things are composed of energy, this energy can be used for either good or bad. Apparently, these primitive methods changed the energy to be beneficial for her, and the ceremony carried my *intent.*

Vicki's Healing

My neighbor Vicki came by one day and asked for help with allergies. She was allergic to tomato vines, horses, dogs, and especially Lysol spray. She worked in a nursing home and every time she used the Lysol spray, her face would immediately break out in a rash.

We went down to the fire circle by the creek and built the usual fire with cedar wood. This was a similar method as with Lisa, except I forgot to tell Vicki to bring any raw meat. I simply took the feather and made sweeping motions around her body and shook the feather over the fire. Then I brought some tomato vines from the garden, crushed them, and rubbed them on her arms. Nothing happened. Next, she petted the dog and hugged the horse, getting horsehair all over her. Still nothing happened.

OK, now for the real test. She had brought a can of Lysol spray with her and I had her spray it in her hand. "Now rub it on your face." I told her. She did and still nothing happened. After 17 years, she is still free of allergies to these things.

Other Healings

One evening we had Georgie, an herbalist, as a guest and had invited several people for supper to meet her. Alicia came with her husband, Gary, and his parents. We had never met before, but Alicia's mother-in-law had asked if I would try to help Alicia. She had had ovarian cancer for about two years. After supper, the entire group made their way down to the fire circle and something strange happened.

My three horses, which had been grazing a quarter mile away, came running up to the group and ran around the fire, bucking and kicking. I wondered about this for a moment and then realized something was causing the horses to do this. Since then, I have observed this disturbance with horses, dogs, and cats when a healing is about to take place. Once, when working with Rolling Thunder in his house to remove the pain from his legs, we experienced a similar incident with his cat. He said that sometimes the bad spirits would cause the animals to do something to disturb the healing process.

Not knowing this at the time, I chased the horses away and

continued with the healing ceremony. Again, I used the feather and symbolically cut her open and swept what I perceived to be the cancer into the fire.

About a month later, Alicia went for a checkup and no cancer could be found. As time went on, we had similar successes with things that hadn't responded to conventional treatment.

I guess what I really learned was a way to symbolically cut a person open and take out the negative energy causing the problem. This can be done a number of ways, as I demonstrate in class.

Once at a party a lady was telling me about having a lump in her breast and asked if I could do anything about it. Taking her aside so we wouldn't be the center of attention, I made a quick movement toward her as if I were reaching into the breast and jerking something out. She felt the breast and her eyes got big and she exclaimed, "It's *gone!*"

About a year ago my friend Teri called for the first time in several months. She lives about 500 miles away and I hadn't seen her in years. In the conversation, she mentioned that there was a large lump in her left breast. We continued to talk and without telling her what I was doing, I imagined her standing in front of me. Reaching out physically with my hand, I symbolically cut a hole in the breast and removed the lump. After a few more minutes of conversation, I asked her to feel the lump. She screamed into the phone, "It's gone!"

Removing pain or sickness at a distance is something we have done for years. It doesn't happen all the time, but many times it works.

Affecting the Weather

Here is a story about affecting the weather with our intent.

Some years back when my daughter, April, was about two and a half, David Bratcher visited us. He was working with Chief

Two Trees at the time and came over to spend the weekend. Since the streams and watering ponds were low, we were concerned about having enough water in our spring. I asked David if perhaps we could do something to bring the rain. There was no rain forecast and the sky was clear, not a cloud in sight. We went up on the hill to do a *pipe ceremony* to bring rain. At that time, April went everywhere I went.

We sat on the ground while David put the tobacco in the pipe bowl. He lit the tobacco and made a prayer to the Spirit of the Rain. He drew on the pipe and blew the smoke into the air. He pointed the pipe stem toward the sky when he did this. He then passed the pipe to me and I did a similar prayer and motion with the pipe. When I finished, April held out her hands to receive the pipe. I passed it to her, and she sat on the ground very quietly and looked as if she were lost in thought. After a few minutes, I reached for the pipe and she shook her head, refusing to give it to me.

I told her, "Just let me know when you're finished."

A few more minutes passed and she pointed the pipe stem to the sky. Then she passed the pipe to me and said, "Finished."

As we got up to leave, I noticed what seemed to be a narrow band of clouds rushing across the sky toward us. Within minutes the sky was cloudy and the next morning it snowed and then turned to rain. In a few days the streams and ponds were full.

Now, there were three of us. Which one brought the rain? Maybe all three, who can tell. But I happened to remember another incident when I asked April, who was then about two, to beat the drum to bring the rain. I still have her on tape beating the drum chanting, "April make it rain." It rained. I suspect that our children could accomplish a lot more if they weren't taught that they couldn't do it.

Not all methods work all the time. People are different and what works for one may not work for another. But then, not everyone can take penicillin. Over the years I have searched for something that will work every time, and I finally found it. Deep in the Amazon jungle lives a tribe of primitive people who have within their culture a belief that when the moon is in eclipse, a jaguar is eating the moon. Traditionally they have performed a ceremony to drive the jaguar away to prevent the moon from being eaten. They build a big fire and the medicine man dances around the fire wearing a fierce mask while the warriors do drumming and chanting. Works every time.

5 Snakes and Their Handlers

One of the things about Rolling Thunder that took me a while to get used to was the fact that he liked snakes. If a rattlesnake came into his camp, he would pick it up and carry it away and would avoid hurting it.

Having grown up in an atmosphere where snakes were low on the totem pole, this took some time to consider. My Sunday afternoon entertainment was to ride my horse along the creek and shoot snakes with a pistol. When I ran out of snakes, Nancy and I would race the horses along a gravel road and shoot beer cans.

Not everyone had the same feeling toward snakes as I did, just seems that I was born with a fear and hate for them, and most people I associated with shared the feeling. Little did I suspect that this would change.

Now, there were groups of religious folks scattered throughout the mountains that had a special use for snakes in their religious services. They had read in their Bible something to the effect that if one had strong faith, they could handle the poison snake and not be bitten, or if they were bitten, they would suffer no ill effects. Some of them were correct; the ones of lesser faith are buried in the customary manner of head to the west and feet to the east. The idea is that when Gabriel blows his trumpet and Jesus comes back, they can rise to meet him and be carried off to heaven. Apparently they expect him to come from the east. They may be right, but I have long suspected that if Jesus were looking for souls to populate heaven, he would choose those with enough sense not to set themselves up to get snake bit.

It has always amazed me that of all the verses in the Bible available to base a religious practice upon, anyone would choose the one about handling snakes. Perhaps this could be due to something called a "self-destruct" mentality. Oh, they practiced the commandment given to Adam and Eve to go forth, be fruitful, and multiply and replenish the earth—but never admitted it.

Now some of these folks took their religion seriously, especially on Sunday. Some would do no work of any kind on Sunday, not even feed their snakes. They would be good neighbors and rational during the week, but in a Sunday service all hell would break loose. Some of the more faithful would even start on Saturday. I have personally witnessed self-appointed ministers capitalizing on the opportunity to address the crowd at the local flea market. They were, for the most part, a pessimistic bunch, dwelling excessively on hellfire and damnation and limiting access to heaven to those in agreement with them. I have often been saddened by this waste of misdirected energy. For, if properly directed, it could have been used to clean up all the trash along the road. There is a tidy sum to be made from these fellows if one could package their enthusiasm and sell it to the government to dispense to their employees. On a hot summer day, their zeal is exceeded only by their body odor.

These references are made so the reader will understand the

dilemma I experienced upon learning that my newfound teacher and friend, Rolling Thunder, was a snake handler.

One thing in his favor was that he had a different reason for handling snakes. He was protecting the snakes rather than making a show of religion. His snakes cooperated better, too.

One day on the way home from work, a snake crawled across the road and I ran over it. No big deal, it was just another snake. But something happened. For the first time in my life, I felt compassion for a snake. The thought came to me that the snake could feel pain and I had caused this pain. The thought also came that if the opportunity came again, I would pass it up.

Guess the spirit world wanted to see if I meant it, because when I got home, there was a snake on my walk. I drew my pistol and started to shoot, but then remembered the promise made a few minutes earlier about passing up the opportunity to kill snakes.

So I started talking to the snake. "You know I don't like snakes and you are in my yard. However, the Creator has placed you on the earth and perhaps you have a right to be here. But I won't tolerate you so close to the house. If you will crawl away, you can live in peace." Walking around him, I went into the house. When I came back out, he was still there.

"Look," I said, "You're pushing your luck. If you're still here when I return from feeding the horses, I will take it as an act of aggression and kill you. If you want to live, you better go." He was gone when I returned.

A few days later, when feeding the rabbits, there was a snake as long as I was at the rabbit cage. He was trying to get at the new litter of rabbits. When one has killed snakes as long as I have, it is just natural to reach for your gun when you see one. But again, I stopped.

"OK, snake, these rabbits are mine. If you are hungry, then go to the barn and catch mice and we will live in peace."

He crawled away. Several similar incidents followed in the next few days. The spirit world was really putting me to the test.

Remembering the story Rolling Thunder had told about making an agreement with poison ivy to prevent it from bothering him, it seemed reasonable to make the same deal with the snakes. One morning I went out in the yard and built a small fire. Taking a handful of tobacco, I addressed the snakes.

"We have been enemies as long as we have been alive. I have killed many of you and you have tried to kill me. Let's make an agreement. All poisonous snakes such as copperheads must stay out of my yard and away from my house. If you will do this, I won't kill any more of you."

I then tossed the tobacco on the fire as an offering to the spirit of the snakes. Something was strange about this fire. The smoke drifted in a 12-foot diameter circle in the grass and never did rise, as is the nature of smoke. I reasoned that it stayed down there where the snakes were.

It was seven years before there was another copperhead in my yard. Before making the agreement with them, I killed several each year.

One night when April was about two years old, we came home after dark. After walking across the porch and turning on the light, I noticed a copperhead coiled on the porch. Rolling Thunder had been very pleased when he learned about the peace made with the snakes, but told me what to do if any of them broke the agreement. I was to make a tobacco offering to the snake and throw the snake over my shoulder and walk away.

April was walking toward the snake and my mind was quickly checking the options. Didn't really want to kill it, but it had broken the agreement. And if April ever got bit, I wouldn't get over it. So I called her to me and said, "April, look at the snake. Notice the color and design of the markings on its body. You don't have to be afraid of it, but you must not go close or touch it. Anytime you see a snake, you must come and tell Nancy or me. Before you were born, I made an agreement with the snakes to stay out of our yard, and this one has broken the agreement and must go join his ancestors."

Whatever I have to kill, I do it quickly. After making a tobacco offering to the spirit of the snake, I tossed it over my shoulder and walked away.

Later, Chief Two Trees and I were discussing this, and he had had a similar experience. He reasoned that the offending snake was not alive when we had made the agreement and that it should be renewed each year.

And then, it has been my experience with animals that some of them just won't listen. I can say for sure the population of snakes greatly reduced after the ceremony. Word got around, and two of my neighbors asked me to talk to their snakes. I did, and none were ever seen around their houses again.

If it weren't for Rolling Thunder, I would still be killing snakes. It's amazing how life changes.

6 How It's Done

David, a freelance photographer, needed to make some money and decided to use one of the methods he had learned in one of my classes. It was a simple enough trick, took little time, and didn't cost anything. All he did was think in pictures rather than words. He concentrated on the problem and visualized a black border or frame around the problem. The way he visualized himself in this situation was with empty pockets. He then destroyed the image and replaced it with an image of one-hundred-dollar bills sticking out of his pocket. Around this image he visualized a bright sparkling white border or frame and it was located slightly to the left of the previous one. Two days later he was hired by a local college to photograph all their sporting events, a position he still holds 12 years later.

Driving through Mississippi late one night, I stopped to fill my truck with gas and add some oil. The oil spilled onto the engine and caught fire. After I got the fire put out, the truck didn't run well enough to continue driving. No help would be available before morning. Getting into my sleeping bag in the back of the truck, I visualized the problem with the black border around it. Then I destroyed the image and replaced it with a picture of driving safely home, putting a lot of white light and energy around this scene. At five in the morning, I woke up with an idea. Raising the hood of the truck, I saw that the accelerator spring had been disconnected. Upon connecting it, the truck ran fine. It may be worth noting that mechanical ability is not one of my greater assets, which adds more reason to believe that these tricks work. But why do they work? Let's consider some other methods before we answer that.

Other Methods

Liz called and was terrified that someone had put a curse on her. There was a fellow whom she believed to be a warlock and wherever she went, he was there. Rather than deal with it, she had chosen to stay home, going out only when absolutely necessary. She asked me if I would come see her and give her some help. Liz lived a good distance away. I drove over one evening and we sat up and talked all night. It seemed like every time we got together, this would happen. She didn't sleep much and wouldn't let me sleep either. At daybreak I told her to get a pencil and paper. "Now draw the picture of what you are afraid of," I told her. "Put feeling and emotion into it."

I stood over her and repeated these instructions over and over, also reminding her, "This is the curse that is upon you." By the time she finished the drawing, she was in tears. Taking the paper and putting it in my pocket, I told her, "Time to go. We have a ceremony to do at sunrise." We went out into the woods and I had her gather cedar wood for a fire. Then we built a small fire. As Liz stood there, I took the folded paper with the picture from my pocket and held it in front of her above her head where she had to look up at it. "This is the monster that has been after you. This is what you fear. This is your curse." I repeated these things a number of times, and then with a swift movement, threw the paper into the fire, telling her, "Watch the smoke as it blows away. It's gone!" To my knowledge, Liz never experienced the problem again.

On a construction job one day, my friend Rick complained of his knee hurting so badly he couldn't walk. I did some of the usual stuff, but the pain was still there. I kept at it until all my tricks had been used up. The pain was still there. Over the years, I've noticed that when we do everything we know how and it doesn't work, it's time to learn something new. Reaching down and picking up a piece of dried mortar, I held it above and in front of his eyes.

"Concentrate on this. It represents the pain in your knee," I told him over and over. "Do you understand this?" When it was clear that he was concentrating on the mortar and believed that it represented the pain, I crushed it right in front of his eyes. The pain vanished.

One more story and then let's see if we can make some sense of all this.

The day I met Valerie was when I walked into the office where she was working. She related a disturbing dream from the night before. In this dream, she and her three-year-old daughter were at Valerie's mother's house, when a big black dog attacked her daughter and chewed her badly. Valerie was understandably upset, as she feared the dream would come true. She wanted to know what to do about it. At the time, she was unfamiliar with relaxation methods and brain waves and such.

I told her, "Tonight when you have put your daughter to bed and all is quiet, sit in a comfortable chair, bow your head, close your eyes, and mentally count backward from twelve to one. When you reach the count of one, remember the dream. Play it out like watching a movie, and when the dog starts stalking your daughter, pretend to pick her up and put her in a safe place. Point your finger at the dog and have him walk away."

Two days later Valerie and her daughter were at her mother's house, and the dog she had dreamed about, but had never seen before, appeared and started to stalk the child. Valerie acted out the role she had visualized earlier and put the child in the car and pointed her finger at the dog, which gave her a surprised look, turned, and walked away, never to be seen again.

Destroying the Form

You may be wondering what all these stories have in common. What is the connection between getting a truck to run, making money, relieving pain, changing a dream, and breaking curses? I am glad you asked.

This is my explanation, as I would deliver it in class. "Many volumes have been written about this and countless seminars given on this topic. I'm going to sum it up for you now and give you the bottom line in seven words. Here they are: *Give it a form—destroy the form!*"

You see, you are creating a mental picture of the desired situation. You are giving energy to it at the most powerful state of mind, and you are actually creating the future event. Remember, you have to *focus on what you want*, not what you don't want. The techniques are just a way to help you do it.

A similar method that works quite well is to let the patient take part in the healing. This has been most effective for removal of pain from the body at a distance. To use this, all you do is give the pain physical properties and give the logical mind a way that it can believe it can remove it.

As soon as I woke up one day, I called Cheryl, who lived about a thousand miles away in Kansas City. "Your back is hurting," I announced.

"My back is killing me. How do you know?" she questioned.

"Because I can feel it. Now, what are you wearing, and what color is it?" I wanted to know in order to have better visualization of her. "I'm going to ask you some silly questions and tell me the first thing that pops into your mind. What size and shape is the pain? What color is it? What does it taste like? What does it smell like? What temperature is it?"

After she had answered all the questions, I repeated her answers. For example, "The pain is the size and shape of a softball, black in color, tastes like mud, smells rotten, and is 100 degrees."

I then described what I was doing. "I'm going to cut the ball in half, then in quarters, then cut it again and again. Now, I'm going to grind it into powder and now that we have a black powder, let's mix some water with it. Stay with me and picture all this in your mind. We now have a black liquid. Now, I am going to take my right index finger and draw a line from the pain in your back down your left leg, across your foot, to the end of your big toe. This is like a transparent tube that will serve as a path for the pain to flow out of your body. I have my left hand in front of your stomach and my right hand behind your back. I am squeezing your body, and the pain, in the form of black liquid, is flowing down this tube, down your thigh, over your knee, down the calf, across the foot and I'm squeezing it out the big toe like milking a cow. Watch it squirt out into the hole in the ground."

"It's gone! My backache is gone!" she screamed.

Getting Information

The more we use our mind, the more we are able to use it. After a while, we start to get information with no logical explanation. An example of this is knowing you're going to have a flat tire. At first I programmed the tire to go flat in a convenient place, such as my driveway or in front of a service station, and this happened. Finally, I got smart enough to know when a tire was going to go flat and prevent it. Once, when Nancy and April picked me up at the airport, the first thing I did was look at the tires. Now this was not something I ordinarily do, but sure enough, there was a piece of metal sticking in the tire. It was a simple matter to get it fixed before it went flat.

Once, when packing for a trip out West, I had a hunch to pack a coil of heavy copper wire. Not having a clue as to why, I put it in the truck. Two weeks later, on the Salt Flats of Utah, we stopped for lunch and noticed six well-dressed men looking under the hood of their car. I considered going over and offering to help, but not being a mechanic, figured I would just get in the way. After about 15 minutes, one of the men came over and politely asked, "We need a piece of extra heavy copper wire for a repair. You wouldn't happen to have one, would you?" The look on his face indicated that he didn't really know why he was asking. I reached into the truck, retrieved the wire, and handing it to him, replying, "I packed it for you and was just waiting for you to ask for it."

Being in the right place at the right time comes in handy. Here's a story from Jim, a guy I met recently. When he wrote to thank me for helping him, I asked him to write a story for the book. I wasn't sure where to put it, but it is too good to waste so this looks like a good place.

Jim's Story

The first time I talked with Raymon, he was responding to an advertisement I had placed to sell my Mustang. Raymon has a very strong personality, and at first I was a little nervous as to where he was coming from. He was full of questions, and not just about the Mustang. I had mentioned that I was out of work on disability, and he started asking me all sorts of questions about my problems. He told me he had "checked me out" and told me a lot of things about myself that were true. Since the call was about selling my car, this sort of knocked me off my tracks, and I suspected he was hustling me.

I figured he had some sort of "spy software" that checks your credit history and such on the computer. It wasn't until later I learned about his dowsing talent. After a bit I realized this wasn't the case, and told him that I had contracted Lyme disease, and it had caused arthritic-like problems in my knees, ankles, and wrists. He said he'd like to try and help me with it when he came to see the car, if I wanted help. I spent most of my life in the Navy as a medic and never believed much in "faith healing" or that sort of thing, but I like to keep an open mind, and he said this wouldn't cost anything, so I said sure.

When he and his friend Debra came, he was as captivating as he had been on the phone. Jeans, boots, drover coat, Stetson hat, and big old skinnin' knife on his belt. I immediately liked him. He checked out the car, then started working on me. He had me lie on my back on my sofa, and went to work. When he was finished, he had me stand up and touch my toes. I did so without any pain. I felt really good, but what really struck me was the sensation of being taller. I had the sensation that the room had lowered, or I had gotten taller.

I hadn't told Raymon, but about 20 years before, while serving with a Marine Corps infantry unit, I had broken a vertebra in my lower back in a helicopter training exercise (I fell out). The vertebra then jumped out of alignment, and made me about an inch and a half shorter. The medical term is a medial subluxation of the L-4 vertebra. This caused a life-long nagging backache. Nothing horrible, but it really slowed me down, and was a constant annoyance. I didn't think to tell him all my problems. My mind was focused on the Lyme disease. I told him this, and he did a little more work on the back. Later that evening, I asked my daughter, Melanie, to measure me, and I had gained back a good inch. The next day I was still feeling good, and when we went to my bank to settle the car business, I left my cane behind twice and didn't even miss it until it was pointed it out to me.

Several weeks later I saw my doctor for routine stuff, and I asked the nurse to measure me. I was back to six feet even. The height I was before the accident. Without knowing, he fixed my back as a side effect! Since then I've read his first book, and am using what I learned to help myself. I still have some pain in my joints, but not nearly as much. And with his visualization techniques, I'm starting to have some real results. I first shake the pain loose, wad it up in my hands, and toss it away. Sounds funny, but it really works.

Thanks, Raymon, I will never forget what you've done for me, and the positive effects you've made in my life. I look forward to your next book.

Prosperity Stories

For years, I have thought that among our greatest assets would surely be our family and friends, and I have used the things I learned to help them. Not all have responded, but enough have to make it worthwhile. It has been obvious that some people will respond to the efforts put forth in their behalf far better than others, but I am not sure why. My Indian friend from British Columbia, Evelyn Rattray, offered this advice: "If your spirit guides don't get along with the spirit guides of the patient, you won't be able to help them." She has been right on so many other things that I see no reason to doubt this.

It also may be that our energy fields are not in harmony with the patient, or they may not be able or ready to receive help for a number of other reasons. The good news is that a great number of friends have been receptive and I would like to call Jeannie back now to tell another story.

One day I was talking with my friend Raymon and we were discussing prosperity. Raymon said he thought we could use metaphysical techniques to improve our prosperity, and wanted to try it on me. I wasn't sure I believed him, but I hadn't been sure I believed in distance healing when he first used it on me, and the results were very real.

So I said, "Sure, go ahead and connect me with the flow of prosperity!"

Unknown to Raymon, I was having a strange problem with my bank. It was time to withdraw money I had invested earlier, but they wanted to pay me less than the amount stated in my original document. I did not expect them to decide the discrepancy in my favor, but two days after Raymon's psychic work, the bank called and agreed to pay me the $4,600 difference. They also asked me if I would mind if they added another $200 because of the way their computer calculated interest! No, I didn't mind! I joyfully reported this to Raymon, but the flow of prosperity was not finished. A week later, a letter arrived in the mail awarding my daughter a four-year honor scholarship covering all college tuition at one of the colleges she was considering. She had not applied for any scholarships, so we were extremely surprised and delighted!

Coincidence? Who knows! Well, Jeannie, as we have said many times, "We make coincidences happen."

An interesting thing about this is that we picked my friend Jeff to be part of the experiment, without telling him. A few weeks later Jeff called and reported that he had received a very pleasant surprise. An unexpected check for $8,000 had arrived. I then told him he had been part of a prosperity experiment. He was most grateful and wanted to be included in any future experiments. Now please don't write or call to volunteer for any prosperity experiments we are doing. All the vacancies have been filled. Just take these ideas and do something like these friends of mine in Omaha did. Here is their letter.

I used some of your dowsing ideas on a car dealership and on the sales people. We were in the market for a new vehicle. We had already been to several dealerships when you were here and had left angry a few times when we were getting jacked around. I did some work on the dealership that I dowsed to be the most affordable/helpful. The end result is, they sold us the car we wanted for a price they said was the *lowest* price they had ever sold that car for. We traded in our old car and got a good price there too. We left feeling happy and they were a little perplexed but seemed content with the whole process. At one point we were ready to sign the deal and they spontaneously offered us another $300 for our trade-in. We had no idea why they did that except for the dowsing we had done. Every time they got up to go talk to a manager, we would be dowsing to make the manager more agreeable. They had no idea what had happened. Arn and I were chuckling to ourselves as we were driving home in our new car. I would say that the dowsing saved us at least $1,000 on the whole deal.

I wanted to thank you for the great gift you have given to us and to tell you that we will keep using what we have learned to help ourselves and others.

Your friends,
Laurie and Arnie Winkelbauer
Omaha, Nebraska

Another Healing Story

Here is another healing story from Jeannie.

In my experience, energy work really can accelerate healing. One morning, I bent over to pick something up off the floor, and couldn't stand back up. My lower back screamed with pain, and I collapsed on the sofa.

Perhaps I was meant to learn a lesson that day. It just happened that a friend was on her way to my house. She had just taken a class in Healing Touch. She arrived in ten minutes, and began to use her new knowledge to work with my energy field. She checked my chakras and found them in bad shape. She worked to clear the energy blockage from my back, but at the same time she urged me to call a doctor. Getting into the car seemed impossible at the moment, so I called Raymon instead. Luckily he was home and was willing to add his healing energy to my situation. After I talked with Raymon on the phone, my friend rechecked my chakras, and found they had become open and balanced. The pain began to subside, and in an hour I was fairly free of pain if I moved carefully. Later in the day, I was able to walk the dog and feed the horses at the barn.

I felt so grateful for all the energy work I had received! I slept without any pain, and the next morning I only felt a small pain when sitting down. I e-mailed Raymon to thank him and let him know I only had a little pain left. As I sat down to my lunch, I noticed that all the pain was completely gone.

I later learned that Raymon had sent me another healing session just about lunch time! The pain never returned, and a few days later I carried some 50-pound bags of horse feed with no problem. In past years, I've had back trouble that took weeks to improve, so I was incredibly grateful for the speed of this recovery and for friends who knew how to help! Without a doubt, there are forces at work in this world that we have barely begun to understand!

Well, I may not understand it either, Jeannie, but one thing seems certain. If we do nothing, nothing will happen; if we do something, something might happen.

7 Introduction to Dowsing

Mary Lou Williams, treasurer of the Appalachian Dowsing Society in North Carolina, invited me to speak to the group at their quarterly meeting. At the time, I knew a little about dowsing, but was unfamiliar with all the things that could be done with it. My talk was to be given on how to expand and use the mind with the methods taught by Jose Silva.

The talk went well and they gave me a year's membership in the society. I didn't realize it at the time, but this was another door being opened. The thing that caught my attention was the degree of open-mindedness these people possessed. Watching the more experienced dowsers work with their whirling pendulums, I was amazed at their ability to get information so quickly, far beyond anything in my previous training. Numerous possibilities began to fill my head. That was several years ago. It hasn't stopped since.

Buying a pendulum, I started to work with it. Things went slowly at first. The thing would hardly move. I would sit for long periods of time and ask questions, waiting to see if there would be a response. Persistence paid off, and as time went by, the pendulum would respond instantly to my questions. The next thing to learn was how to ask questions, since the greater amount of our success depends upon asking the correct questions.

An excellent book for the beginner is called A *Letter to Robin* written by my friend Walt Woods. In this little book, Walt does an excellent job providing information to get started. My progress would have moved much faster if I had known about the book. The book also has a chart of numbers around a circle, which can be used in many ways to get information. By wording a question precisely, you can get information in the form of a percentage. We will go into this in more detail later. Walt has made this available for free at www.letter torobin.com

Dowsing is a method that has been used for centuries to find water, and there were a few people in the mountains here who possessed this skill. To my knowledge, that was about all they ever did with it and there was little understanding of it. They knew that if they held a forked stick of a specific tree and walked over a vein of underground water, the stick would point downward to the location of the water vein. This was so amazing, although still not believed by many, that no one seemed to look for any further possibilities.

Of course there were always a few of the righteous who denounced it as "the work of the devil." Once, when word got out that I had performed a healing ceremony on someone, it wasn't long before I was accused of "working for the devil."

My response was, "That's not true. I'm self-employed."

Actually, my differences with some of the ultrareligious folks have been mutually beneficial. My ideas and work have provided the ministers with numerous sermons and they have provided me with some good writing material.

How to Do It

As near as I can determine, the dowsing instrument is simply a tool that gives a physical response to confirm what we already intuitively know, but don't know that we know. It is my belief that the power that moves the dowsing instrument is the same power that causes the wind to blow and the rain to fall. If this is true, then we are in contact with universal mind, higher consciousness, God, the Great Spirit, or a higher power—by whatever name.

Again, let's give attention to those who would want to give the devil credit for this work, for in their minds, the devil has many disguises. It seems fair to determine whether something is good or bad, positive or negative, by the results it produces. If pain is removed, peace and love are restored in the family, alcohol use is lessened, abuse is decreased, and some women don't get the hell beaten out of them anymore, this seems to provide sufficient evidence of the source of the power. When this type of work is attacked by the ignorant and self-righteous, it causes me to be suspicious of whom they work for.

Now, let's get on with the dowsing. It is generally known that one can get responses such as "yes" and "no" from the use of the pendulum. We may have our various ways of determining the responses, but the end result is the same. For example, to indicate a "yes," the pendulum may swing in a clockwise manner for one person, but for me it swings toward my body, then away from it. A "no" response for some will be a counterclockwise swing, but for me, it is a swing across my body from left to right.

To count something on the chart is easy. Just predetermine if you are counting in units, tens, hundreds, thousand, or millions.

You will notice that there are two circles of numbers on the chart. For the most part, the numbers on the outer circle are ten times greater than those on the inner circle. In other words, they have an extra zero.

And how do you know which circle of numbers to use? You ask. For example, I used this in counting a herd of cows for my friend Don Yows, who was 1000 miles away. He had sent me an e-mail asking me to do this because he had to fill out some type of forms for the government. For some reason, they wanted to know how many cows he owned. There was a blizzard and he couldn't get out to count them.

Using my pendulum and chart I asked, does Don own more than 30 cows? Yes. Does he own more than 500 cows? No. This told me that I would use the outside circle of numbers because they ran from zero to 500. I then asked, "How many cows does Don own?" The pendulum swung between 50 and 60. I then went to the inside circle and asked, "Fifty and how many more?" The pendulum swung to seven. Don had 57 cows.

After the blizzard was over, he counted them and confirmed the answers were correct. There was only one problem. I had counted three dead cows. I hadn't asked how many *live cows* Don owned. Take note and be careful how you ask the question.

When looking at the chart in the book, you will notice a minus sign on the left and a plus sign on the right. This is the minus and plus quadrant of the chart. The numbers 1 through 10 can be used as percentages—1 being equal to 10 percent and 10 being equal to 100 percent. This is useful in determining the value of food or drink upon your body. You can just ask, "What is the overall result of this [name the food or drink] upon my body?" Then watch to see where the pendulum swings. If it is on the plus side, it can be reasonably assumed that it is good for you. If it is on the negative side, it isn't. The same method can be used for any medicine or supplements. It can also be used to determine the honesty of a person. You might find it interesting to use it to check on your elected officials or other powers that be.

Frequencies

Now is as good a place as any to tell you how I prevented the accident with Larry mentioned in chapter 1. Remember, I had gotten a flash or mental picture of his car colliding with a truck. I simply used the pendulum to scramble the frequency of the accident. You see, everything seems to have a frequency. There is an ideal frequency for the human body and there are frequencies for diseases. I had been working with this for a while, so I figured there was a frequency for accidents. I had learned that it was possible to scramble the frequency of a disease and have it disappear. Now this has not happened consistently, but it has happened enough to keep doing it.

I work in a real simple manner. If a technique works for one problem, I will use it for something else. It is my nature to take whatever information is available and apply it to benefit my family and friends. One of the first things I did was an experiment to determine if healing at a distance could be done with dowsing. You see, dowsing not only gives you answers, it can be used to send energy, or carry your intent. One night Mom called, and as we talked, without telling her, I checked on what I refer to as a "pain level." Hers was in the "discomfort range." How did I know this? Well, I was measuring it on the chart from 0 to 100, and it measured about 20. You can give anything a numeric value and then measure it with dowsing.

After a few minutes, Mom asked, "What are you doing to me? My back stopped hurting!"

Let me say this before going further. There are some specific procedures to follow if you want to get the correct answers. It is a good idea to ask for permission to get accurate information. Ask if you have the ability to work on the particular project, and ask if it is the appropriate time to do so. This can be shortened to "may I, can I, and should I?" I usually follow it up with, "Is there any reason not to?" In addition, I always ask for the help of my most appropriate spirit guides. It is most beneficial to reach a state of relaxation, as we discussed in chapter 1, as this will help put your mind on the frequency to obtain correct information.

If you get a "no" on any of the questions, then it is worse than useless to proceed. Try again later because conditions may have changed.

How and why did the pain leave Mom's back when she was unaware of any treatment being given? It couldn't have been power of suggestion because there wasn't any. It couldn't have been her belief, because she hadn't asked for help or mentioned the pain. So, what caused it? *Intent!*

Once the level of pain had been recognized, I respectfully asked for the pain to be lowered and removed. The pendulum swung in a counterclockwise manner for several seconds and stopped. It was then that Mom discovered that she didn't hurt any more. It was my *intent* to remove the pain. Dowsing with a pendulum was the vehicle to bring it about.

If we can observe the movement of a dowsing instrument when we provide no muscular effort on our part, then our logical mind can more readily accept the idea of help from somewhere else. There is something involved here besides the physical world as we know it. It seems that when our intent is good, the spirit world will cut us some slack. That is true in the beginning because they probably want us to be encouraged with our success and go on to learn something else.

Every healing trick has worked for a while and then it was time to learn something new. So it was with lowering the pain level. After a while, it became necessary to address the cause of the pain. This is still evasive, but there were certain things found that could be corrected.

As I said in the foreword, "We are the sum total of our heritage and our environment."

If we have inherited the color of our hair, eyes, skin, and body type, then we must also have inherited the beliefs, thoughts, and memories of our ancestors. This isn't so strange. How many times have you heard expressions like, "Kidney stones, heart disease, baldness (or any number of other things) run in the family"? Then why can we not have memory of events and conditions of our ancestors?

I also said, "We may be stuck with our heritage but we can change our environment." Well, maybe we can change our heritage too.

I progressed to the question, "How many beliefs, thoughts, and memories are there that adversely affect this condition?" Then asked, "What percentage of them are inherited and what percentage are self-imposed?" There is usually a very high percentage that have been inherited. How do we change what we have inherited?

If everything is composed of energy, as we discussed earlier, then beliefs, thoughts, and memories must surely be energy too. If energy can be changed into different forms, then why can't we change it to something more beneficial? We refer to good and bad energy, but is it really that way, or is it neutral energy being used in a positive or negative way?

There seems to be a way to change this and we do it by asking to remove the emotions from the beliefs, thoughts, and memories of the person we are helping. This is how we neutralize the energy that has been used in a non-beneficial way. The pendulum will swing counterclockwise until this has been completed and then reverse its spin to clockwise. At this time, we have neutral energy, ready to be transformed into something beneficial. Ask for the energy to be transformed into the most appropriate energy for the highest good of the person. It's what I call "mental judo." Does this work? The people who get well think so.

Jakie's Story

Let me give an example. Jakie, a friend of mine, and I were talking about how we both sometimes have aggressive tendencies.

We assumed this to be a characteristic of our Irish heritage. It serves a purpose, but at times can be detrimental at social events. Whenever one draws a pistol and shoots out the lights, his name is customarily stricken from the guest list.

I was explaining the previous information and he readily agreed to offer himself as a candidate. We had another friend whom we chose to rehabilitate as a service to humanity. We agreed to tell him later if it worked, and if it didn't, we would read about it in the local newspaper. We thought it advisable to include me in this project also.

We first counted the number of beliefs, thoughts, and emotions each of us had that contributed to aggression. If it had been a contest at the county fair, I would have won a blue ribbon. Next, we asked to remove the emotions from all these and transform them into the most appropriate energy for our highest good.

A week later Jakie and I talked. We both were in a better mood but it was about a month before I talked with our other friend. I asked him, "Have you felt as aggressive as usual in the past month?"

He thought for a moment and grinned, "No, come to think of it, I haven't. What did you do to me?"

This indicated a couple of things. One, it worked. Two, it worked even if the person didn't know about it.

Allergies

I found it also worked on children. Remember Vicki, the young woman who was allergic to Lysol, dogs, horses, and tomato vines? That was about 17 years ago. Now she has a 13-year-old daughter and a 5-year-old son. We talked one night and she reminded me of working on both of her children. At five years old, the daughter, Tracy, had allergies I assumed to be inherited from Vicki. At two years old, her son, Shawn, had asthma and the doctor advised that it looked like it would be a bad case of it.

Vicki brought both these children to me, about five years apart. On Tracy, Vicki reminded me that I had put my hand over her chest and had told her that I was going to pull something out and had run my finger down her arm. As my hand reached her fingers, her eyes had gotten really big and she had felt something being pulled out of her fingers.

Shawn was a different case. First, I checked him for the usual beliefs, thoughts, and memories and changed the energy of them. Then Vicki reminded me that I put my hand on his chest. Neither of the children has had any problems since.

You may be asking why I didn't change the energy of Tracy's beliefs, thoughts, and memories of the allergies. Simple, I didn't know how at the time. This brings up a previous statement: "If you have good intent, the spirit world cuts you a lot of slack."

Questions

OK, here are some questions that I have been asked concerning this:

What did I do to these children? Well, once the number of beliefs, thoughts, and memories contributing to allergies was identified, I neutralized them.

How? By use of the dowsing system. The pendulum would swing to the appropriate number, indicating the number of beliefs, thoughts, or memories adversely affecting Shawn. Once this was done, I asked to neutralize the offending items and the pendulum spun in a counterclockwise manner.

About putting my hands on them? Well, laying on of hands has been a form of healing for a few thousand years.

Did I impart some miraculous healing energy to them? Maybe.

What qualified me to do that? I wanted to help them.

But who ordained me for such work, what papers or degrees do I have? Didn't know I needed anyone, degrees, or papers.

There are two kinds of people—those who doubt, ask questions, but never accomplish anything. Then there are the kind who believe—or at least want to believe—and *do something!* Which one are you?

More Stories of Allergies

A few years ago, a group of parents invited me to Alaska to teach a class for their children. These children stayed with each other quite a bit and slept at different houses, usually wherever they were at bedtime. One 11-year-old boy got left out a lot. He was severely allergic to cats and most of the people kept cats in the house. I liked this kid and wondered if there was something to be done. I used the dowsing to make the changes, neutralizing the energy causing the allergies, and transforming them into a strong immune system. Also did something else.

It seems that time exists only in the physical world and we are working in realms other than the physical. I asked to be able to go back in time before he was born and change the makeup of his DNA in such a way as to enhance his immune system. In addition to this, he also learned how to program himself to improve his immune system.

With all this done, his confidence was high and he went to spend the night with someone who kept cats. The cat slept with him that night and there was no allergic reaction.

Since then we have had success helping many people with food allergies. Here are a few examples.

While I was visiting friends in Texas, it was brought to my attention that one of the women had allergic reactions to wheat and dairy products. This seems to be a common problem. That night, after working with her, we went out to eat, and as a test, she ordered spaghetti with cheese sauce, which had always caused a problem in the past. No problem.

In a class in Florida, a lady had a terrible reaction to kiwi fruit. Her mouth would erupt in blisters if the raw fruit touched it. We did a mass healing for the entire class to eliminate their food allergies. The next day someone brought kiwi slices for snack time. She tried tasting one and there was no reaction. When I returned six months later, she was still able to eat kiwi with no problem. This is the most dramatic reaction yet on food allergies.

How was this accomplished? Simply by using the dowsing system to neutralize the ill effects of the offending food upon the person.

I cannot say to what extent this can be effective and these examples are not to encourage anyone to take dangerous risks by consuming any substance known to be harmful to them. (Remember the snake handlers? Same principle applies here.) It does, however, show that in many cases people have the ability to change the effect of food upon their body, which may improve the quality of their life.

These are three stories from Lydia in Florida, who had a most unusual experience. Her life changed overnight from being filled with fear, to confidence. When she later hosted a workshop for me, she handled it like a professional. She took what she learned and is using it to make a positive difference for other people. Here's Lydia.

Lydia's Story—#1

During the year 1998, health problems began to seriously limit my activities and by December I was unable to continue working. From June of 2001 to the end of January of 2002, I was in the hospital four times with ovarian surgery and heart and respiratory problems. My nerves were extremely bad and I had a fear of people; therefore, I became, for the most part, a recluse.

My friend Nancy, from near Charlottesville, Virginia, suggested I call Raymon, because he had done some work for her. We were on the phone for 33 minutes and he finished by saying, "You should sleep better tonight." I wasn't aware of a difference until the next morning when I walked outside. It was as if my spirit had been imprisoned in my body and now all the walls came crumbling down. My energy body was huge beyond belief; it was literally reaching at least the size of two football fields. In one direction I saw the lake, only this morning it wasn't at a distance—I was experiencing the water as if I were physically in it. The immobilizing fear was completely absent; the powerful presence of my spirit knew fear was no longer part of my reality. Physically I was experiencing something akin to weightlessness, yet I felt so big I would allow a greater distance when I was in the presence of anyone because I had the feeling I would actually bump into them. This tremendous presence of spirit required getting use to and I found myself using caution when others were near. This must be what one experiences when they make the transition to spirit, only then learning who they really are. Thanks to Raymon and the spirit world I didn't have to wait.

Needless to say, after this experience, I wanted to meet Raymon and be taught by him. I was probably a pest about him coming to the area, but he did agree and came May of 2002 for a workshop. We have since had him back again for another workshop, which has given us tools to help others and ourselves.

Lydia's Story—#2

There is a group of us that meet every other week to use Raymon's techniques and learn from each other. One night during one of these meetings I got a call from a lady (out of state) who was desperate to get in touch with Raymon for help with a legal session taking place the next morning. I didn't have much hope for her reaching Raymon, so I told her that we as a group would see what we could do if she could give me a few necessary details. It concerned a male friend of hers who was being taken unfair advantage of. There was to be a meeting with the divorced husband and wife with the attorneys at 9 A.M. the next morning to sign the final agreement. The husband had already lost 80 percent of his assets to this woman he had been married to for only three years (no children and both professionals) and she was going for the rest of them. Our request was for spirit world to intervene and cause fairness to be accomplished. We also ask that greed and evil intent not succeed.

Three days later I get an e-mail from the lady explaining the circumstances of the meeting. At 9 A.M. all were present when the ex-wife walked in with a disabling headache saying, "Show me what to sign." She signed and stomped out. The attorney said, "I can't believe she signed this agreement; I am happy, now it is fair." We thought it significant the attorney used the word *fairness* since we had asked specifically for that to take place.

Lydia's Story—#3

One evening my friend Nicole called saying she was ill, couldn't get warm, hurt all over, and had been in bed for hours that day. She agreed that we use dowsing to see if it would help. I asked that her brain and her entire body down to the cellular level be cleared of all programs, thoughts, beliefs, and memories of disease. The pendulum moved for a considerable amount of time and shortly she said, "Lydia, I am getting so warm, I have to take my jacket off." The next morning she was completely recovered.

Marilyn's Story

Here is another story written by Marilyn Gang. This story took place about eighteen months after her first story.

"Creating Positive Energies and Achieving the Results You Want"

The Toronto Dowsers is a group I started in September 2000. As of this writing, two years later, we have monthly meetings that attract over 120 people a meeting, we have a membership of over 200, and we send out a monthly newsletter to over 300 people. We have just changed our meeting location to a room that holds 380 people. I think we are going to need it. I don't think it's a minor "coincidence" that I got the idea to start this group a week after I met Raymon at the June 2000 ASD convention in Vermont.

The Consumer Health Organization of Canada (CHOC) is a fine, national non-profit organization that works to encourage the prevention of disease through knowledge and to educate the public about holistic and alternative health choices. They have a convention, the Total Health Show, at the Metro Toronto Convention Center in the spring. These shows attract thousands of people.

When I told them about Raymon Grace, they enthusiastically agreed to have a booth for the Toronto Dowsers and for us to sponsor two presentations by Raymon at their annual show in March 2002. When I discussed the plans for the show with Raymon, I asked him to please use his dowsing ability to help us have a good location at the show.

When we came to set up our booth at the show, we found that we had *the* best location of all of the booths! His first presentation was well attended. His second was packed. We must have reached a thousand people that weekend. Something big was started.

I had been feeling quite drained of energy that Sunday and didn't take the time to do anything about it or ask for help. About

10 P.M. that night, at home, I could feel a lifting of the heaviness and a great increase in positive energy. I knew that Larry and Raymon were driving home from the show at that time and that they were working on me.

When I spoke to Larry the next day I said: "You and Raymon were working on me between 10 and 10:30 last night, right? You found something, what did you find?" He told me they found some curses put on me from someone we knew. I often know when they are working on me because I can feel a heaviness lift and evaporate. That person never bothered me again.

We continued to experience beneficial results. At our February 2002 meeting, we had a lot of new people. Larry was the speaker and 135 people showed up. Many had not been to one of our meetings before; they did not know how to dowse and perhaps thought they were going to learn there. There was a lot of scattered energy. Word had started to spread about the work Larry and Raymon were doing and people came to be "fixed." This is one of the unfortunate side effects. People come expecting to be "fixed" when what we are trying to do is to teach them the techniques so they can do this for themselves, their families, and friends. So a lot of the walking wounded showed up. We don't want patients or takers. We want givers, students, and teachers. I had neglected to ask for good energy and so left to itself, like a boat without a rudder, the energy was fractious and all over the place. At that time we were not used to so many people and it was difficult to handle it.

I knew that Raymon's presentation at our following meeting in March would attract even more people and wanted to ensure that energies would be more harmonious. I asked Larry to create the energy for a meeting where "people would be interested, capable of understanding and using the techniques, and would add to the group." Two hundred and fifty people showed up at that meeting. We all felt that the energy for the humongous March meeting was "one-derful."

Afterwards, I thanked Larry for his help. He told me he didn't do a thing! I told him I saw him work on it. He said he only checked to see if he needed to do anything more. He said I did the whole thing by my *intent*. We now do an energy clearing and energy raising the night before each meeting. Things are changing in positive ways for our group.

Doing this is fabulous. Look at what each one of us can do! Knowing Raymon's techniques, and not using them, is like someone offering you a million dollars but you say, "No thank you, I'd rather remain poor."

Marilyn Gang

Leader, Toronto Dowsers

www.TorontoDowsers.com

mgang@dowsers.info

Dowsing has also been very useful in helping change the behavior of kids gone astray. One evening at the Canadian Dowsing Conference, Larry and I were met by a couple who needed to talk. We were on our way somewhere, but after listening to them a few moments, we decided talking to them was more important. We are glad we did, because over a year later, this is their story. As you can see, this was worth whatever time it took.

Abigail's Story

We feel it is important to tell this story about our daughter, Abigail. She, like many teenagers, is going through a very difficult period. Abigail was very depressed and questioning staying on the planet. She was not communicating with us at all and was in and out of high school. We had exhausted a lot of possibilities with counselors and medical help. We were out of answers and did not know where to turn. June 2000 we met Raymon Grace and Larry

Huszcco and with Spirit's help, connected at the appropriate moment in time and told them what was happening with our daughter. Raymon and Larry immediately started to dowse for her. The results started immediately, as the next morning Abigail asked what we had done because she felt a lot more hopeful and positive.

We continued to use Raymon's methods and experienced dramatic results. Abigail is now completing high school and will probably go on to a university. She is now dowsing and even showing her friends what dowsing can do for them.

We have also worked with many other teenagers and have experienced positive results. We truly believe that by actively dowsing, all things are possible.

Bruce and Robyn

Bonnie's Story

Here is a story from my friend Bonnie in Omaha, who became an excellent dowser after attending a class with me. I read this story to most of my classes to inspire them to use what they have now, and not wait until they have all the answers.

I started dowsing in September 2001, the first evening of a three-day workshop with Raymon. I decided to attend the class because I was interested in energy healing and had read that Raymon had studied with Native American medicine men. I knew nothing about dowsing. At the end of the first day I walked into the store next door, bought a pendulum, went home, and copied the *Letter to Robin* off the Internet. I then started practicing by dowsing food, to determine its nutritional value. This was a trick Raymon taught us in class.

By the end of the three days, I started dowsing for my family, friends, and myself every evening after work. I would routinely go into the silence of the "Medicine Place" [another technique I learned in class] and developed a connection with the spirit world. Right away, I noticed a difference in my moods and knew that if I felt off balance or irritable, I could change it, in minutes, with dowsing.

My first noticeable success that involved another person was influencing my 13-year-old son to improve his grades in school. Without my saying a word to him, he went from failing grades at the end of the first quarter in math and English, to B grades at the end of the second quarter.

Since then, I have improved my own health, influenced the healing of my son's injured knee, removed various aches and pains from him, and have changed anger and respect levels to maintain harmony in my home. As I write this I'm beginning to realize how long the list of improvements and changes is. Here are just a few of them: quieting and calming crying babies; getting a parking space close to my office, even at the busiest time of day; ending non-productive conversations without saying a word; clearing up acne; relieving headaches, arthritis and other painful symptoms; assisting the healing of broken bones; and reducing or eliminating emotionally related problems.

I have been able to use dowsing to stabilize my emotions during a death in the family. I also used it to improve the actions and personality of a man who was not treating his family very well. Being able to dowse has improved my life a lot.

Bonnie's comment about dowsing the nutritional value for food was a result of a story I told in class about April. When she was about 11, she wanted a soft drink. I knew the nutritional value of this was a minus 45 on the scale. I said, "I'll make a deal with you. If you can raise the nutritional value of this drink to a plus 70 you can have it."

She took her pendulum and swung it over the drink for a minute or so, intending to raise the nutritional value of it. Then she brought it back to me. When I checked it, I found it to be plus 90.

A few days later she was eating a cookie. I said, "I didn't see you raise the nutrition of your cookie."

She replied, "I don't have to."

"Why?" I wanted to know.

"Because I have programmed myself that everything I eat or drink is good for me."

I haven't been able to prove her wrong.

8 Bill and Winnie

It is not always easy to know when someone will have a great influence on us. The best way to handle this is to be nice to everybody.

In 1995, I was invited to speak at the Silva World Convention in Laredo, Texas. This was an annual event, held each August and hosted by Jose Silva. Silva Method lecturers and graduates from all over the world gathered there to hear a variety of speakers and to socialize. A highlight of the convention was the awards ceremony where lecturers were recognized for various types of achievement. Having won a couple of awards previously as Outstanding Lecturer of the United States was probably the reason for me being invited.

I invited my friend Gary Robinson, who had excelled in the use of the information he learned in the class, to go with me. In fact, I had invited him to participate in the talk I was giving, since he had used some of the techniques in ways no one else had heard about. We were looking forward to the opening night of welcoming festivities, which by my standards was a formal affair. In anticipation of such an event, I had worn my best boots and jeans!

The ballroom was filled with people and there were about 25 countries represented at the opening festivities. While most were socializing around the punch bowl, I was just observing the people. By now, I was fairly well known here, since this was my fifth visit, and many people came to speak and shake hands with me. The others probably wondered how I found my way to town.

Besides myself, all in attendance were well dressed in suits and nice dresses. That is, all but two. It appeared that a good time was being had by all. All but two. These two were sitting, backs against the wall and very alert, smiling at everyone. The problem was, no one smiled back. No one even looked at them. For all practical purposes, they weren't there.

This hit me the wrong way. This was an organization reported to be a guiding light for humanity and these people were being ignored. It was time to do something about it. I walked over, introduced myself, shook hands, and invited them to attend my presentation on using the Silva Method for healing purposes. They introduced themselves as Bill and Winnie Askin from High Level, Alberta. His business card read, "The Old Trapper and The Woman—Professional Hermits. Don't call us, we'll call you."

They seemed like my kind of people so I spent as much time with them that weekend as possible. Gary and I would visit with them at every opportunity and eat with them in the dining room.

Bill and Winnie had taken the Silva class in Canada and had also studied other types of mind development. They were well read and carried on a most interesting conversation concerning dowsing and energy work. They had flown to Laredo to attend this convention and meet Jose Silva. At the time, it seemed a bit odd for a couple of trappers from a remote area of Canada to be here at a place like this. But then, I was from the remote mountains of Virginia, and I was here. When I asked more about where they lived, Bill replied, "The last house before you get to Russia."

The main thing I noticed about this couple was, they were *real*.

Bill bought tapes of my talk at this convention and apparently passed them out all over Western Canada. Later, I received a letter from Bill written on notebook paper with a pencil. He described himself as "a bushman by trade." For 18 years he and Winnie had operated a trap line in Northern Alberta near the Northwest Territories border. They spent months alone in the winter, working in 40-below weather, miles from another human. In another letter, he made reference to energy, saying, "In the cities, very little has meaning. Out here in the wilderness, everything has meaning. The energy has not been polluted."

Letters turned into phone calls and a friendship developed.

One day Bill called and asked, "If we were to buy you a plane ticket, give you a place to stay, and feed you, would you come up here and speak at our conference?" This was a "Power of Thought" conference that Bill and Winnie were strongly involved in promoting. It was scheduled to take place in July of 1997. Bill asked if I would talk about healing and give some information on how to do it. In addition, I was to visit with others at the conference and, hopefully, answer any questions on the subject.

I learned later they had watched me perform healing work on someone in Laredo. Their main objective was to enlighten people so as many people as possible could have a better quality life. After deliberating a couple of seconds, I answered, "Yes."

He described his request further by saying, "Now, you won't make much money, but look at it as a mission. We need someone like you up here."

I replied, "I don't know why you need me, but the answer is still yes."

Never having been to Canada, I was wondering about the procedure for getting to Hay River, Northwest Territories. I called a friend who owned a travel agency to inquire about a ticket. When they learned where I wanted to go, they said that in all their years of business, they had never sold a ticket to that place.

My concern was getting through airports, as I had limited experience with such things. I had always made it a policy not to go anywhere I couldn't drive my truck or ride my horse. Memories of an old man from the mountains came to mind. When I was a boy, he visited my grandpa and told me a story of the time he moved from the mountains where we lived to a place near Roanoke, Virginia. Each morning he watched a bus pass his house and each evening he watched it return. He suspected it was going to Roanoke and decided to catch the bus one morning and go to town. Sure enough, as he stood by the side of the road the next morning, the bus driver stopped to pick him up. When he arrived at the bus station in Roanoke, he noticed there were several other buses there. He wondered if he'd know which one to get on to return home at the end of the day. Being resourceful, he tied a string to the door of the bus he arrived on so as to be able to recognize it later. Unfortunately, when it was time to leave town, the string was gone. He became confused, got lost, and it took him three days to get home.

I knew a better plan was needed so I called my friend Jeff Jones and asked, "Would you like to go to Canada for two weeks?" Knowing few details, he agreed. He was a good traveling companion—agreeable, adventurous, and knew his way through airports. He had a unique characteristic. He almost never ate. Oh, maybe a few peanuts or some popcorn every few days. During the entire two-week trip, he ate one cracker. But he drank water, about a gallon per day.

You see, Jeff had taken a class from me and learned a trick that he turned into something the rest of us hadn't thought about. He figured he could "program" the water to contain all the nutrients his body needed. The peanuts and popcorn were mostly to satisfy his craving for salt. Now a number of people, including doctors, have been in classes with us. These people were far more knowledgeable on the requirements of the body than Jeff, and they knew it wasn't possible to live on water alone. The problem was that Jeff didn't know this. It seems that his body didn't know it either. Jeff simply visualized the water as containing all the nutrients needed by his body. Well, if everything is energy, including our thoughts, then why not?

Boarding the plane in Tennessee was no problem because it was a small airport. Following Jeff's advice, I had left my gun with Nancy and April, who had taken me to the airport. I packed my belt knife in my duffel bag to be checked in as luggage. In my backpack were my usual items for surviving in the concrete jungle: water, energy bars, dried fruit, nuts, toilet paper, powdered drinks, cup, eating utensils, can opener, my home-made fire starting kit, and camouflage pants and shirt. I was also able to get my Swiss army knife through the security check point.

We flew into Salt Lake City and from there on to Edmonton, Alberta. Flying with Jeff had its advantages. He knew his way around the airports, how to find the correct gate to board our plane, and since he didn't need food, when meals were served, I ate his lunch.

Flying from Edmonton, Alberta, to Hay River in a small plane was quite an adventure. The pilot let me sit up front between him and the copilot. This was indeed the best seat in the house! My eyes tried to take in everything. There were miles and miles of trees and lakes with no sign of human habitation. Occasionally we would land at a remote airport to take on or let off passengers. However, this airport was quite different from others we had traveled through earlier. Everyone was plainly dressed and just walked out to the plane and got on. Flying was the main way of travel in a land where there were few roads. At one place the pilot, copilot, and all passengers got off the plane and walked into the airport for a short break. Everyone was friendly and made Jeff and me feel welcome.

When we arrived in Hay River, Northwest Territories, Bill and Winnie met the plane and took us to the campground where the conference was to be held. Bill is very plain spoken. His advice was, "Leave most of your stuff here and get in the truck. We're going somewhere." Leaving my duffel bag in a teepee and taking only a change of clothes and toothbrush, we got in the truck to go "somewhere." Where? Jeff and I had no idea!

"Somewhere" turned out to be Yellowknife, capital of Northwest Territories, which is north of the 60th parallel. Only one road goes there and for miles it is a dirt road. A map of Northwest Territories shows Yellowknife to be at the end of the road on the north shore of the Great Slave Lake. I remembered the flyer advertising the conference. Among other things, it said, "Those traveling from the south will have a paved road all the way." Such a statement suggested those traveling from other directions would not have a paved road, and this was true. Road construction was in progress and in many places we drove around and through mud holes.

Bill's truck was a four-wheel-drive Ford diesel extended cab with a camper large enough for comfortable travel. He and Winnie lived out of it several weeks during the year and it was large enough for Bill, Jeff, and me. We would stop from time to time to look at a lake or large waterfall and take some pictures. At one point we stopped to let a herd of 57 buffalo cross the road. They were in no hurry and milled around the truck for quite some time.

After we continued several more miles north, Bill pointed to an old, abandoned cabin, telling about an old Indian who once lived there. Further on he pointed out some simple crosses about 30 feet from the road, making comments about those buried there. Once we stopped to talk to a road construction crew and Bill knew some of them. The thing about all this that amazed me most was the fact we were about 300 miles from where he lived! At noon Bill pulled the truck to the side of the road and announced, "Time to eat." We climbed into the camper and Jeff and I sat around the table while Bill took bread, cheese, tomatoes, potato salad, moose roast, and homemade raspberry jam from the refrigerator. Food supply didn't seem to be a problem; neither did time.

After driving on for several more hours, we camped overnight by a lake. Camping consisted of eating supper, washing the few dishes in the little camper sink, and getting into our sleeping bags and going to sleep.

This far north it doesn't really get dark in July, so I drifted off to sleep in the twilight. We were up early the next morning and I had a bath in the lake listening to the cry of a loon. While standing knee deep in the lake, the realization came to me why people in the North Country may not learn to swim. The water is cold!

This trip was one of the highlights of my career. Life has never seemed the same after this experience.

We reached Yellowknife late the next morning and it became clear that Bill and I had a similar phobia, cities. Yellowknife was not a city by standards here in the States, but it had buildings close together and traffic. Some of us just never seem to be comfortable with those conditions. Bill's friends Dave, Martina, and their nine-year-old son, Kevin, lived here and we parked in their yard.

Bill mentioned a restaurant where he wanted to take us, so we invited Martina out to lunch. The restaurant, Wildcat Cafe, was built of logs in 1936 and would probably seat at least 35 people. The menu listed caribou burgers. I will make comments later about my being a vegetarian, but that day I was on vacation. I learned caribou has very little fat, no added chemicals or growth hormones, and can be quite tasty. Having had the foresight to purchase some Canadian money, I gladly treated my friends to lunch.

Dave, Martina, and Kevin were wonderful hosts, taking us places and making us feel at home. Martina had reserved a room at the local library for me to speak in that evening.

I asked, "How many people are expected?"

"Maybe eight," she guessed.

Sixteen people showed up. I spoke on the possible uses of our minds for 30 minutes, thanked them for their attention, and sat down. As a group, they informed me, "You're not finished yet, keep talking." So I kept talking for another hour or more. Then we visited and answered questions for another hour. After that, some of them followed us back to Dave and Martina's house, where we were staying. We continued to talk to them and treat them for aches and pains for a few more hours.

The word got out and three full carloads of people drove 300 miles south to our conference scheduled for three days later. Since then, Bill has gone back to Yellowknife to teach a number of classes. I began to suspect this was the "mission" he had in mind when he invited me.

The next day Dave drove us to some of the local lakes and waterfalls. The scenery and energy of these places was unlike anything I had ever experienced. The country consisted of large rocks, evergreen trees and lakes clean enough to drink from.

As we left Yellowknife a day later, Bill asked Dave to help us get out of town. Dave obliged by leading the way on his bicycle, all four blocks.

After driving about an hour, we met a car. About 20 minutes later we met another one. Bill turned to me and said with disgust, "I don't know where all this traffic is coming from. It didn't used to be this way up here!"

At noon we stopped to have lunch again and by and by a truck came along. The driver stopped to ask if we needed any help. The driver worked in the oil fields and he and Bill visited for quite a while. The fact that they didn't know each other was of little importance. We offered him lunch, but he had already eaten.

Again, I noted the difference in people here. In the States, I have been stranded on the side of the road with a breakdown while thousands of cars went by and no one stopped.

Time seemed to mean nothing. We stopped to camp overnight on the Mackenzie River and took a picture of the sunset at 11 P.M. The picture still sits on our fireplace mantle.

Arriving at the conference site in Hay River, we began preparing the facilities. Bill had made arrangements with someone to "build" the tent. Small trees had been cut for tent poles and rafters. A tarp was used for a roof and we were in business. Someone had brought several folding chairs and others used their own.

The location was at a campground in a bend of the river. There were sufficient outhouses, two cold water showers, a teepee for my headquarters, and, as a bonus, several saskatoon berry bushes and an organic garden.

Saskatoon berries grow on bushes so low you can reach the top of most of them. They resemble blueberries and were so abundant that a gallon could be picked in only a few minutes. Each morning I would pick a pailful for the kitchen, a plywood structure measuring approximately 20 by 30 feet. It was equipped with electricity, some type of stove, and long tables. The owner of the campground assured me it was OK to take all the berries and vegetables from the garden that we needed. In July the garden consisted of onions, spinach, and other types of greens. This was my kind of place! There was no doubt in my mind that I had arrived!

The only thing needing improvement was the weather. It was cold and raining and almost time for opening the conference. It seemed something should be done about the rain. Memories of a story told to me by Chief Two Trees came to mind. It was hay-cutting time and Chief and some farm help were baling hay. The sky was dark and thunder could be heard in the distance. The helpers were expressing their fear of the hay getting wet and spoiling. Chief told them not to worry, just keep working.

"But it's going to rain," they protested.

"No it isn't," Chief insisted, "Keep working."

When the hay was baled, Chief told the helpers to come back in the morning and put the hay in the barn.

"But it will be wet," they continued to protest.

By the next morning it had rained on all four sides of the hay field, but no rain had fallen on the hay. This story amazed me and I asked, "Chief, would you mind telling me how you did that?"

"Stuck an ax in the ground," he replied.

"I sure appreciate you sharing those words of wisdom with me, but I fail to see the connection," I answered.

"Oh, you have to use a double-bit ax," he explained. "One blade of the ax goes into the ground and the other blade points up to split the clouds. It is your *intent* that does it."

Nothing ventured, nothing gained. Going around behind the teepee, I planted the handle of a knife in the ground with the blade pointed at the sky. Addressing the Spirit of the rain, I asked the clouds to split and let the sun shine through. Then I visualized the sun shining. Just as we were walking toward the tent, the clouds broke and the sun came out. Did I do it? I don't know, but if you don't believe in what you're doing, you should get out of the business!

A number of things caught my attention at this conference. About 70 people had come from as far as a thousand miles away. They had traveled some of the distance on dirt roads, which was evident from mud on the cars. Nearly everyone pitched in to help with the chores. But what really got my attention was that Bill and Winnie had put most of it together by themselves. Many people contributed food. Winnie and a few other women in the kitchen prepared meals for most everyone.

There were about a dozen speakers at the conference, each speaking on his or her field of expertise ranging from Native healing to alchemy. The Native healer was Evelyn Rattray from British Columbia. We became good friends and still are. She is mentioned elsewhere in this book.

After the conference was over and the teepees and tent were taken down, we drove about 230 miles back to the Askins' house. Winnie went on ahead in the car while Bill, Jeff, and I followed in the truck. The only bad part was the mosquitoes. Those things could bite through clothing, and did so without hesitation! We built a smoky fire to keep them away. By the time we arrived at their house, there were already about 25 people in the yard. Some had tents set up and some had campers. Bill and Winnie hadn't been home for over a month, but you couldn't tell it. Things progressed as if they had been at home all day waiting for the guests to show up.

The house was made of wood with thick walls and roof for good insulation. There were two large rooms separated by a curtain. One room was a kitchen and dining area. The other was a combination bedroom and living room. Tanned furs from a variety of animals adorned the walls and furniture. Bill had built everything of wood and coated it with a clear lacquer so that the walls shined. I used up a roll of film taking pictures of the place!

I might add, they lived about 30 miles from town or anything else and had no running water or electricity except from a solar energy system that provided lights. A wood stove provided heat in the winter and a propane stove was used for cooking. Propane was also used to operate the refrigerator and freezer.

Water was obtained by melting snow in the winter and catching rain in the summer. There was a gutter on the house that transferred melted snow and rainwater into barrels. Bill always needed to be home during the spring thaw to fill these water containers. He had several 55-gallon barrels and I noticed one plastic 250-gallon tank. I also noticed that the water tasted fresh and asked how this was possible. I remembered as a boy, one place we lived had a cistern that collected and stored rainwater. That water tasted terrible! Bill explained that he used a weak solution of food grade peroxide to keep the water fresh.

Bill and Winnie's house also had something on the windows I hadn't seen before. It was very heavy wire mesh. They said its purpose was to keep the bears out of the house.

This might be a good place to add that in the city, people can go to work, do as they are told, and get paid. The utility companies will send them bills and all they have to do is write a check to pay them. Someone is usually making their choices for them and as long as they have a paycheck coming, someone will tell them how to spend it. If they have an emergency, they can just dial 911. Out here it is different. To survive here you must be able to think. If you make a wrong choice, you may not get a second chance.

Jeff and I pitched in to help by picking raspberries. As we filled the containers, it occurred to me that I hadn't carried a gun for almost two weeks. I mentioned this to Jeff and he responded, "I haven't carried one either and don't even miss it."

This place was definitely having an effect on us. It may be help-ful to explain that carrying guns was a part of the world I lived in. This was one of the few places I had ever been without one. Carrying guns was an accepted practice among most of my friends back home. We had the belief that free men did not need permission to carry guns. For if we needed permission, then we were not free.

I recall an incident once when a friend of mine was invited to go to church with his girlfriend. He had visions of sitting on a back seat, but they arrived late and all the back seats were taken. The sermon was already in progress as she led him toward the front of the church to be seated in the front row. As he sat down and leaned back to make himself comfortable, his pistol fell from his coat pocket and slid across the hardwood floor toward the pulpit. He did the only thing reasonable under the circumstances. He just walked over, picked it up, blew the dust off of it and replaced the gun in his pocket. It took the minister a few minutes to regain his composure, but then it was business as usual. He did say that thereafter his girlfriend never again insisted they sit on the front row.

Having spent a lot of time as a kid with my grandpa's old buddies born in the late 1800s had its effect upon me. Growing up with those old men who lived in a world that no longer exists caused me to look at life differently than most people liv-ing today. It was believed that when the government removed the people's right to bear arms, they created slaves. I hadn't adjusted well to modern laws and ways of life.

I cannot prove or disprove these figures or source, recently quoted to me, but I quote them out of concern for safety of the reader. These figures are supposed to be from the U.S. Department of Health and Human Services.

• There are about 700,000 physicians in the U.S.

- There are about 120,000 accidental deaths caused by these physicians each year.

- There are about 8,000,000 gun owners in the U.S. That is 8 *million.*

- There are 1,500 accidental deaths caused by guns each year.

Is it reasonable to conclude that guns are safer to have than doctors?

Back to Bill and Winnie's—a bucket of water was brought in, vegetables and berries were picked from the garden, a caribou roast was put in the oven, visitors brought in some food, helped in the kitchen, and in a short time, dinner was served.

Nancy became a vegetarian several years ago and since she is the cook, April and I also became vegetarians. This wasn't a bad thing. No animals had to be killed, we ate healthy food with no growth hormones or additives, and believed we were better off for it. I had gotten on the vegetarian bandwagon. However, I was quick to discover that Winnie's caribou roast can cause one to fall off the wagon. I haven't decided whether Jeff has a lot of will-power or his taste buds are dead!

Their garden was nothing less than fantastic! We have a garden, one of the better ones around, but Winnie's garden was something else. Everything was mulched, no weeds were present, and vegetables were much bigger than any I had ever seen. And Winnie hadn't even been there for a month!

I wondered what kind of fertilizer or nutrients they used. *Energy!* Bill had a device rigged up that fertilized the garden from outside the garden and did it all with *energy.* He called the device a "cosmic pipe." It consisted of a ten-foot long piece of PVC pipe, about four inches in diameter. There was a rock the size of a cantaloupe held on top with duct tape. Bill said that at the base of the pipe there was some fish emulsion, trace minerals, and a coil of copper wire. It seemed this device would broadcast energy to the garden, providing needed nutrients.

He also had some things he called "rock devices" that I would call "medicine wheels" scattered over his property. These were rocks placed in a circle, some weighing over 500 pounds each. He said these produced a healing energy and God only knows what else.

Winnie also told us of the "little people" who lived in her garden. She could see them. They were small and wore old-fashioned clothes. Noises frightened them and when Bill came too close with the tractor, they would run and hide under the cabbage leaves. Once, on Bill and Winnie's way home after a long absence, they came to meet the car and were so glad to see her that they danced on the seat!

Bill also told of a winter night when the Northern lights were quite active. Winnie beat on the leather-covered drum and the Northern lights came down around the cabin.

After supper, Bill took us out back to a cabin. His traps, wolf hides, beaver pelts, snowshoes, and assorted trap-line gear were hanging on the wall and there was a kerosene lamp. "This is your house, hope you like it." In my travels, I've stayed in a lot of places, good places, but I have never felt more at home than in this cabin.

As the days flew past, there were many activities and lots of visiting. Evelyn, the Native healer, and I did some healing work on those needing it. Evelyn is one of the best healers I have been privileged to know. Healing ability runs in her family. Her grandfather was a medicine man. She has a most effective method of helping people release pent-up emotions of grief, fear, sexual abuse, and a multitude of other things that many people carry to their graves. I was honored when she asked my help and offered to teach me how to do the work she does. We made a good team, each complementing the abilities of the other.

(Two years later I invited her to come and spend a couple of weeks with us. I had arranged for a few speaking engagements for her in three states. She and Marge, her traveling companion, were well received at all places she spoke. We invited friends for a gathering and picnic and drew people from eight states. Afterward, there was a steady stream of folks coming to receive treatments from her for a week afterward.)

Word got out that we were there and other people came to us for help. There was an assortment of folks from far and wide—professional people, laborers, Indians, and another trapper and his wife who came for either visiting or healing. One Indian woman we had helped brought her daughters and neighbors to see us.

Gradually the people drifted off on their journeys home.

One of the more significant friendships I established was with Karen Embree from British Columbia. She was attending the conference with her sister, Ann, and friend, Shirlyn. Afterward, they had decided to "travel with the circus" and followed the group to Bill and Winnie's place. (Since then she and I have camped in the Yukon and British Columbia.) She has been a wonderful friend.

Many lasting friendships had been made and leaving wasn't easy, but we had a plane to catch. As we boarded the plane to fly south, I thought again that my life would never be quite the same.

As soon as I got home, I started building a cabin like the trapper cabin I had stayed in. There were a number of reasons for this. One was that our house is small and we needed a guesthouse. Bill and Winnie were coming to visit us in about a year. I had just about finished the cabin when Bill called to say they would be here the next day.

"Good," I said, "Your house is almost ready. I put a coat of varnish on the floor today."

There was a pause, after which he replied, "For many winters we lived on the trap line in a tent with a dirt floor."

Bill and I had been discussing energy for quite some time and he was giving me an education on the subject. At the time, I had no idea of the significance of this information.

In December of 1997 Bill called to tell me he had discovered an energy unlike any he had previously experienced. He could measure it and noticed it had an effect upon people. He not only could measure it, but could influence it. When the energy got too high and interfered with his activities, causing a lack of focus, he simply lowered the energy.

In most every audience I've spoken to in the past two years, I've asked this question: "How many of you have recently experienced any of the following symptoms? A vibration in your chest similar to an adrenaline rush or as if you had drunk too much coffee, lack of ability to focus your thoughts, or disrupted sleep patterns." Most hands in the audience will go up.

These seem to be symptoms associated with the rising energy when the (I will use the term "Earth energy") is higher than the energy of our bodies. We have learned to raise the energy of the body appropriately higher than the energy of the Earth.

Bill began to use the dowsing system to foretell where the energy would spread next. He predicted it would arrive in my area of the country in September of 1998.

What was this "energy"? What I am going to say here is the way it looked from where I stood. As long as I had known Jose Silva, he had made reference to "the second phase of human evolution" and had predicted its arrival. I am not sure if he knew exactly when it would arrive or even the specifics of what would happen. He insisted that people would need to learn to use both sides of their brain and know how to use the alpha brain wave frequency.

Someone told me that Edgar Cayce had predicted that the "Christ Consciousness" would come to earth in September of 1998. (I have not verified this.)

The flower children of the sixties sang about the "Age of Aquarius."

Bill Askin had found a "new energy" on the Earth and was able to measure and use it.

Were these people all referring to the same thing? Was the *second phase of human evolution,* the *Age of Aquarius,* the *Christ Consciousness,* and what we referred to as the *new energy* all the same thing? I thought so.

In September of 1998 the *energy* arrived in our part of the country. So did Bill and Winnie. I suspect they brought it with them. Never have I seen anyone as energy sensitive as these two. Bill told me he can feel the energy of a city just by flying over it in a plane. Most of the references to measuring energy in future chapters of this book will be a result of conversations with Bill and Winnie, which continue until the present time. They have had more influence on me than they suspect and will probably only be aware of it when they read this.

One day during a walk in the woods with Bill, I rolled a log into a gully. "I do this to prevent erosion," I said. Bill's response surprised me and I've never forgotten it. He said, "If you would teach one person to do what you do, it would be worth more gullies than you could fill in a lifetime."

Let's back up a bit. Shortly after meeting them in Laredo, I received a call from Harold McCoy, founder of the Ozark Research Institute in Fayetteville, Arkansas. Harold asked if I would come and teach for the ORI at one of their Power of Thought Schools. I was honored, but couldn't help asking, "Why? You don't know me!"

His reply was, "No, but Bill Askin does. He sent us a tape of a talk you made and recommended you."

The tape was a recording of the talk I gave in Laredo. Never did I suspect it would reach so far or so many! I accepted his invitation and have been invited back a number of times since. This has been, and continues to be, a door opener to many good people and opportunities. I will have to say that Harold and Gladys McCoy provide the best information at the most reasonable price I have found anywhere.

One day a call came from a representative of American Society of Dowsers asking if I would speak at their national conference. "I'm sorry, but I have already accepted an invitation to speak in Canada," I answered.

"Oh," she responded, "Bill and Winnie must have invited you. Please give them my regards." It was becoming evident that Bill and Winnie were known in places outside the bush country of Northern Alberta!

I doubt that the people who attended the Silva World Convention in Laredo in '95 will remember the two people sitting against the wall smiling at everyone. After all, they didn't look very important. They will never know what they missed!

Those wishing to contact Bill and Winnie, send a self-addressed stamped envelope to:

Bill and Winnie Askin
P.O. Box 339
High Level, Alberta TOH IZO
Canada

9 Water

Five years later life had changed considerably. During those five years, I had visited Northwestern Canada each year to speak at various conferences. These visits had been wonderful opportunities to stay in touch with friends and make new ones. Even though Bill and Winnie had attended the same conferences and we had opportunities to visit, I hadn't been back to their house. We had kept in touch by phone about every two weeks. We were continually learning and making use of what we learned.

During this time, Larry Huszczo had become my traveling partner for all of my Canadian trips and most of those out West. You remember Larry—he is the one who had steel plates in his back and they disappeared. Well, Larry and I had been working together on a regular basis and he had become an excellent dowser and healer. He had also become vice-president of the Canadian Society of Dowsers.

Time had come to go back and visit Bill and Winnie again, and I asked Larry to go with me. We stayed in the same little trapper cabin that I had stayed in five years before. Several old friends came by to visit as well as some new ones. Among the long time friends was Joan, a Royal Canadian Mountie, and her dog, Toby. They stayed and traveled with us for about a week.

In preparation for our gathering, Larry and I helped Bill tie ropes to the trees to support several tarps that served as a roof over the food tables. This was to protect us from both the sun and the rain, and they came in quite handy, since we experienced both weather conditions. It was quite useful in keeping the rain from soaking the potato salad.

On the appointed day, several people showed up carrying food, and we had a feast. After dinner, I made a talk on some of the work we were doing, and shared healing information with the folks. We would also work with some of the people to do whatever we could for them. It was a *people helping people* event. This event was repeated at least three times that week.

One of the people who attended each event was Branht Allen, one of the neighbors. Branht was a young fellow, 22 years old, and he dressed about like I did, with his boots, hat, and big belt buckle. I'm sure he would have worn a six-gun if it had been legal. Something about him was different. Now this is not to insinuate that there was a normal one among us, but Branht was still different. He was extremely interested in healing work. He reminded me of myself, several years earlier. Anyone who really wants to learn in order to *do*, impresses me. I really don't care to talk to curiosity seekers. Branht took the information offered and began to use it on his family and came back for more.

Seemed like he was a good investment in time, so I autographed both of my books and gave them to him as a gift to get him started. He gave me a Marty Robbins CD to listen to as we traveled. He was one of the few people who liked the same kind of music as I did—old gunfighter ballads. (We have since made tapes of our music and exchanged them through the mail.)

Branht's Story

Branht didn't fool around waiting for all the answers. He used what he had at the time. Here is a story about some unusual dowsing that he did.

Seems he and his dad had an old 1952 D7 Caterpillar bulldozer that wouldn't run. Bill had told him to find the problem by dowsing. This was to be done by holding the pendulum in one hand, while putting the other hand on various parts of the engine. When the pendulum started to swing, that would indicate the location of the problem.

Good idea, but Branht didn't have a pendulum handy when he went back to work on the bulldozer. He had a hunch that the problem was in the fuel pump. He just put his hand on the fuel pump and could *see* the pendulum swinging in his mind. He told his Dad to remove the cover from the pump and it was obvious that a pin was missing. Replacing the pin solved the problem.

As Branht and I talked one night, he told me of increasing the metabolism for his mom and dad to help them lose weight. He says it is working.

I am going to have to go back and visit him someday. He was teaching Larry, Joan, and me to lasso and we enjoyed the lessons.

Anyone wishing to write Branht, here is his address:
Branht Allen
Box 1165
St. Paul, Alberta T0A 3A0
Canada

The Water Project

We had taken on a number of projects and seemed to be making progress on them. I could probably write another book on the projects but will only write about one of them now. This was our *water project.* I had been giving thought to this for years and finally reached a point where we could actually do something. Here are a few simple facts that everyone should know, but live as if they don't know.

Each day there is less drinkable water on the Earth. Each day there are more people drinking and polluting it. This is a trend that cannot continue indefinitely. It may continue until there are no humans left to pollute it.

It can, and is, getting worse. Think for a moment. If you are old enough to remember, in 1973 the price of gas went from about 30 cents to a dollar a gallon very quickly. At that time would you have believed that 30 years in the future, you would be paying as much for drinking water as you would be paying for gas? Only a very few far-sighted people would have realized this. But today it is a reality, not just a bad dream. How much will you be paying for it in another ten years? Will it be available at any price? Will your children and grandchildren even have a decent drink of water? If you want a shocking peek at one man's look into the future, I suggest you read *The Quest* by Tom Brown, Jr., who is mentioned elsewhere in these pages.

We now have evidence that we can do something to change what may seem inevitable. Again I quote my friend Don Yows, "Keep on doin' what you're doin' and you'll keep on gettin' what you're gettin'." Here are some stories to share with you, and like the other stories, this is the way we see it from where we stand.

For several years I had been conducting an experiment with those attending my classes. Someone would put a glass of water on the table and, at my request, the dowsers in the class would measure the energy field of the water in the glass. By energy field I mean the distance from the glass that the energy of the water could be detected with a dowsing instrument.

With most water from a public water supply, the energy field was about five to six inches. I would then take the glass of water in my hands, following a Native American ritual of offering it to the four directions, and ask to increase the energy field of the water. The water would then be set back on the table and the dowsers would measure it again. This time the energy field would be as much as 70 or more feet.

Once I gave the water to a person in the audience to drink who was walking with a cane. The next day she came looking for me to say that there was no more pain in her leg. She had driven herself to class, rather than have someone else bring her as had been necessary before. She left her cane at home.

Now this was always a good attention getter and it was effective in demonstrating the power of thought. Those attending the class were always encouraged to use this method to energize their drinking water. But so many people want someone else to do it for them. After all, they have been taught in various ways that they don't really have any power of their own. There have even been some that come to me afterward and ask if it would be OK if they did this to help their children. Like they *needed my permission!* This is how we know people have given away their power, or else it has been stolen from them. It is their water, their thoughts, their children, why do they need permission from me or anyone else? Take what you have and *use it!*

Now those of you with more education will demand scientific proof, because that is the way you have been trained to think, and dowsing doesn't offer scientific proof. Well, it took a while, but now we have it—that is, if you will accept a water analysis report as scientific proof. I received a request from California concerning a polluted well. The lady making the request said the water had been tested and was too polluted to drink. She asked if I could help lower the pollutants in the water. The only thing I knew to do was to scramble the frequency of the pollutants and adjust them to the frequency of pure water.

Six weeks later, the water was tested and it contained only one half of the pollutants. Four weeks later, the water was tested again and the pollutants were again reduced by one half.

On the way home from Bill and Winnie's, Larry and I stopped to spend the night with our friend Michael Stodola in Saskatchewan. Michael has a giant labyrinth he has built, which measures 85 feet in diameter. He hauled in 120 metric tons of sand for the base and then placed 58 metric tons of boulders to form the labyrinth. You can see it at www.ablecrystals.com.

Michael was telling us about his well that contained a high level of arsenic. He had a filtering system to take some of the arsenic out of the water but it still did not reduce the amount of arsenic to an acceptable drinking level. According to the information he gave us, the *filtered* water still contained 46 parts of arsenic per liter.

As with many cases, we really didn't know what would happen, but wanted to help. We scrambled the frequency of the arsenic and adjusted it to the frequency of pure water.

About three months later I got a very exciting call from Michael, telling me that the lab had sent him the results of the water test. The *unfiltered* water now contained less than seven parts of arsenic per liter.

Now you might ask, why was there any arsenic left in the water? Who knows? Maybe we just need more practice. I'm thankful that we were able to change it as much as we did.

Walter Huszczo

Let me introduce you to Larry's Dad, Walter Huszczo, who is quite a thinker. He had designed several "energy structures" from metal. Some of these are fairly large, measuring ten feet or more from one side to the other. He has also designed some smaller ones to be placed inside the house. The term he uses to describe them is *sacred geometry*. He has them sitting around his place in the house and yard. Yes, they do produce energy.

He had these structures at the University of Toronto, where the Canadian Society of Dowsers Convention was being held. One, which he calls the Flower of Life, is a seven-foot diameter ball, constructed of copper tubing and over a mile of twisted copper wire. He designed it so the top half could be lifted, allowing a person to step inside with the aid of a ladder. Once inside, the ladder was removed and the top half could then be lowered, enclosing the person in the Flower of Life. This allowed the person inside to be completely surrounded by the energy produced by the structure. His experiments with this indicated that an energy was produced that seemed to remove a great amount of pain from many of the people who took the opportunity to stand in it for a few minutes. During the whole weekend event, people would stand in line to have their turn at standing in the Flower of Life. Many of them experienced a reduction, or complete absence, of pain after standing in the structure for a few minutes.

An interesting thing about this Flower of Life structure is that Walter consulted some engineers to get information about building it. They told him that such a structure could not be built. There was nothing left for him to do—*he built it anyway*.

Energizing Water

On one of my visits to his home, Walter asked me to help him with a water experiment. He had six bottles of water that had been energized by various means. One contained the famed healing water of Lourdes in France.

He asked me to energize a bottle of water for the experiment. Walter had the bottles numbered, and on a piece of paper, wrote the number and information identifying the type of energizing the water had received. He put the paper in another room so I couldn't tell which bottle we were testing. He then asked me to pick a bottle and put it on the table. Walter would go to the end of the hall and walk toward the water with his dowsing rods. Where the rods crossed was the edge of the energy field of the water. After it was tested, I would then tell him the number of the bottle and he would record the distance of the energy field. Neither he nor I knew the source of the energizing of the bottle we were testing.

All the energizing of the water worked. No water had an energy field of less than ten feet. The healing water of Lourdes went out about 20 feet. The water I had energized went out about 60 feet.

I asked Walter to test the energy field of his swimming pool that was filled with water from the well. His dowsing rods crossed at three feet from the edge of the pool. Walter suggested that I pour the bottle of water I had energized into the pool to see if it would change the energy field of the pool. I suggested that we only use one drop to see what would happen. Dipping my finger in the bottle to get one drop hanging on that finger, I put my finger in the pool. I then stirred the water a bit with my hand and asked Walter to measure the pool again, but to start farther away. He went out over 60 feet and walked toward the pool with his dowsing rods. At about 40 feet the rods crossed, marking the edge of the energy field of the pool. From three feet to 40 feet with only one drop of water! This got us excited.

Then I noticed the Flower of Life sitting a few feet from the pool. One of those rare brainstorms hit. Without telling him, I mentally put the Flower of Life in the pool and asked that the healing properties and energy of the Flower of Life be transferred to the water. Then I asked him to go way out in the yard and slowly walk back to the pool. The rods crossed at *200 feet!*

We were even more excited but didn't realize what had happened. We didn't realize it until a week later when we were at Bill and Winnie's. Walter called to tell what had happened. He had burned his arm and the wound had not healed. After being in the pool for a while, he noticed that the wound was completely healed. Being a benevolent soul, he invited his neighbors to come and experience the pool to see what would happen. Seems like the aches and pains were left in the pool.

There were seven of us together that night. Bill, Winnie, Bob and Carol from Ohio, Joan, Larry, and I. I went outside and filled a bottle of water from the water barrel. Bringing it inside, I asked Bill to check it on a scale that he called a Bovis scale. Now, I had heard of this but was not familiar with it. Using his dowsing rod, Bill determined the energy of the water to be at 2,000 on the Bovis scale.

I took the bottle of water and after offering it to the four directions, asked for it to duplicate or exceed the energy of the water in the swimming pool. Bill tested it again and it appeared to be at one hundred thousand on the Bovis scale. We then passed it around, each one energizing the water with their own method. Bill again tested the energy of the water. *One million!*

Now Winnie had been experiencing a sore ankle and my attempts to remove the pain had been unsuccessful. This had bothered me, and I didn't understand why it hadn't worked. But now we had more tools to work with. I asked Winnie to get a pan large enough to put her feet into. While she was doing this, I held the water and put a "thought form" in it. Now a thought form is nothing more than a mental picture of your intent. As soon as I finish this story, I'll tell you another one about a thought form.

Winnie took off her shoes and socks and put her feet in the pan. I poured the water in the pan and she exclaimed very excitedly, "The water feels like it's moving up my legs into my whole body." In a few moments, she noticed that her ankle didn't hurt anymore. That was the thought form I put into the water; it did exactly what it was supposed to do.

Another interesting thing happened; we checked the water a few days later and the energy had *doubled*. A few more days and it had *doubled again*. Then the energy seemed to taper off. This was very similar to the energy of the Earth after the "energy raising" on September 22. This will be discussed in chapter 13.

Thought Forms

Now, about that thought form. Seems like a farmer, right across the road from Larry's place, had spread chicken manure on his field. Maybe you city folks don't know what this means, but farmers spread animal manure on the field as a form of fertilizer, and it has a terrible odor. Larry and his folks could hardly breathe. Jannette, Larry's mom, created an imaginary wall, two hundred feet high, as a thought form. The purpose was to stop the odor of the chicken manure from coming onto their property. It worked. A neighbor from a mile away was visiting one day and questioned why the odor was so strong at his place but there was none at the Huszczo farm.

Now you know about thought forms and you know thought forms can be put into water. And you know that your body is composed of mostly water.

Is a light starting to come on?

Back to Bill and Winnie's cabin and the water. We energized more water that night. One of the thought forms we put in it was that the water would affect any other water it touched. It would transfer the properties of the original water to the water it contacted, and the process would be repeated as many times as possible. There may have been a better way of wording it, but that was the best we had at the time. We were leaving for a

1,500-mile road trip and along the route, a few drops of water were placed in major rivers and lakes.

Now, there seems to be an individual in a group from time to time who likes to ask useless questions. Questions like, what studies had been done and what verification did you have that this was valid? How did you know it would work in running water? How can you evaluate the long-term implications of your actions? Did you have written permission of the proper authorities and was it notarized? If so, what is the expiration date? I have a blanket answer for people with questions like this. "Either lead, follow, or get out of the way."

Surface Tension

A few months later I was visiting the Huszczo family and Walter asked me to help him with another experiment. We had learned a bit about the surface tension of water. Our information indicated that water needed to be at a measurement of perhaps between 45 and 48 dynes to carry the proper nutrition to our cells and to carry the waste material away from the cells. A dyne is a unit of measurement to determine the surface tension of water. Previous dowsing had indicated that 47 dynes is the ideal surface tension for my body. In checking a few other people, it seemed that there was a slight difference in the ideal surface tension for different individuals.

Walter set a cup of water and a bottle of water on the table and asked me to check the surface tension of each of them. The water in the cup was 87 dynes and the water in the bottle was 45 dynes. This puzzled me, and I asked Walter where the water came from.

He said, "The cup of water came from the kitchen sink and the bottle of water came from the grocery store."

"OK, 87 dynes is reasonable for well water, but what about the 45 dynes in the bottle from the store?"

Walter then told me something he had been holding back. "The bottle of water had been sitting in the Flower of Life."

"OK, but why 45 dynes?" I then checked to determine the ideal surface tension of water for Walter's body. Guess what, 45 dynes.

It became obvious that we were dealing with a high level of intelligence. Can this intelligence be directed, with our intent, to serve a useful purpose in cleaning up the water? We think so. Is it teachable to other people? We think so.

Coliform

Shelly was in a class in Toronto, which was sponsored by the Toronto Dowsers, and she took the information seriously. She was able to reduce the coliform in a well for one of her friends. The amount of coliform was 780 before testing and 49 after testing. This was tested before and after by the Ontario Ministry of Health and Long Term Care, Laboratories Branch, Bacteriological Analysis of Drinking Water. The world needs more people like Shelly. She *did something.*

These stories aren't just for entertainment. They are for information. Information that you, the reader, can use to make a difference in the future of your life and the lives of your descendants. We all drink water, and our bodies are composed of water. This will be true of your descendants.

Experience has taught us that most people won't do much without encouragement. Numerous people have asked me to energize water for them to help get started. At this writing, efforts are starting to provide water that I have energized to be made available to those who will use it to heal the water of our planet. Here is part of a recent leter from my friend Don Scott of Richmond, Kentucky. Don is a retired minister who attended my class and started using the information to help people in his congregation. He has some wonderful successes; here is one of them.

Hi Raymon—

Just wanted you to know how well the energized water works. I bought a 20-gallon fish tank in January. I have not been able to clear the water because my tap water is so full of rust and iron. I have stopped drinking or cooking with it. I used the recommended treatment and nothing worked. The fish were dying. The fish were attacking and chasing other fish and I was ready to start all over again with a new batch. Then I spied the bottle of water that we all purified when we dowsed for your water project. I gave each of them a small jar with tap water in it from the church to dowse after we dowsed to purify the water around the globe. I looked up all the pollutants on the internet to name them specifically so we would not miss any. I gave them a dropper with the instructions to use this to purify the tap water they use at home. I put a dropper of water in the 20-gallon tank. I sat down and read my mail and in about an hour I happened to glance over at the tank. The water was crystal clear, the fish were swimming lazily around the tank and not attacking other fish. No more fish have died. It is still clear as a bell and I just sit and marvel over it.

Your friend,

Don

I would like to conclude this chapter by encouraging you to teach your children to respect water. This is one of our problems: Most people today were never taught to respect the natural things that are necessary for our survival.

Here is a story I wrote in the summer of '88, one of my "Letters to April," written in a notebook with a pen.

April, it has been said that man is the only creature who will leave the earth in worse shape than he found it. I would like to be an exception to this and assist others in the same endeavor.

We were at a reunion this past Sunday. It was held in a small park in Lebanon, Virginia. There were several people there in addition to the kinfolk. There was a small creek flowing through the park, and I noticed that it was clogged with trash. This consisted mostly of cups and paper plates thrown in the creek by various picnickers.

There was no excuse for such behavior, as trashcans were provided. Why people would pass up a trashcan in favor of the creek has puzzled me. Apparently they weren't taught to respect the earth. Maybe they hadn't given thought that regardless of technology, their existence depended upon water to drink. It has been said, "If you think education is expensive, consider ignorance."

You and I got some trash bags from the truck and proceeded to pick up the trash. You were very helpful and soon we had the creek cleaned. As we worked, people began to stare at us, like they were wondering why anyone would do such a thing as pick up trash—*on Sunday.* We made a good team, kid; you were too young to notice the stares and I was too old to give a damn.

After cleaning the creek, you kept saying, "Daddy, want to play in it!" My mind drifted back almost 40 years, and memories of how much I liked to play in the creek filled my mind. But at a gathering such as this? With everyone wearing their Sunday clothes? Well, it was just not proper. So with these thoughts in mind, I removed your shoes and socks. I watched with deep satisfaction while you waded in the creek, threw rocks in it, and sailed little sticks, which became imaginary boats. You had the time of your life while another rule of society bit the dust.

10 Raising Energy

While Bill and Winnie were visiting us, we rented a nearby school and invited like-minded friends who came from several states to join us. It was more than a social get-together, it was to educate people to some possibilities. The folks brought food for a picnic. Bill taught an excellent class and it was a day of fun and learning to measure energy.

Once we learned to measure the energy, the next step was to influence it. If all things are composed of energy and we can influence it, it seems that we would be able to influence events. For our measuring, we used a chart from the *Letter to Robin* book mentioned earlier. Since we didn't know just what to call these units of energy, we didn't call them anything. If the energy is at 8,000, is it fair to ask 8,000 what? I don't know. It's just a way to measure something I can't define. If we can't define it, then how do we know it exists? By the results produced. Sometimes when working on a problem for someone, I find things that are harmful and know how to remove them, but don't know how to define them. So it is with this energy. We can measure it and influence it, but not define it. I realize most writers would consult the dictionary on such matters, so I did. It didn't help. What did help was to know how to do it. We do it just like splitting the clouds, with *intent*. Here again, we have tools to help with our intent. The tools are the pendulum or a flexible rod called a bobber. These are just devices to help us focus our mind.

Perhaps it is time for a story to help the reader make some sense of all this.

One night Bill and I were discussing some problems I had been working with in a town about 200 miles away. I could correct the problems, but in a few days they were back again. It seemed as if some black magic was being used on some of the people in the town. After measuring the energy in the town, Bill's comment was, "If we raise the energy high enough, the black magicians will not be able to practice."

Let me say here that it is not necessary to be physically present to measure the energy of an area. It seems that the energy can be both measured and influenced at any distance.

As an experiment, I picked up the bobber, in this case an 18-inch copper wire with coils on the end near the handle to make it more flexible. Facing toward the town with the bobber held in front of me, I mentally stated my intent to raise the energy in the town. What happened next was a total surprise and not yet fully understood. The bobber began to move in a manner that appeared to be drawing symbols in the air. It was swinging wildly and my arm was being moved by it. This went on for several minutes.

As Bill watched, he exclaimed, "I've never seen anything like this!"

I sure hadn't! It was my first experience at any of this. After the symbols had been drawn by the bobber, it then swung in a clockwise manner for several more minutes. Then it stopped. The show was over. We still didn't know what had happened.

Next night a call was received from a friend who lived in the town.

"What are you doing to this town?" she asked

"What makes you think I'm doing anything?" I answered.

She replied, "Because more people are smiling and cheerful today. I can feel a difference in the energy and I knew you were up to something."

Needless to say, this got our attention. We hadn't told anyone what we had done. No plans had been made. We just tried something and it worked. Would it work again? What else could be done? We intended to find out.

Over the next two years I performed a similar experiment before several hundred people at various locations across North America. In every case the energy was raised to a level where most, if not all, of the people in the audience could feel something happening. In some cases they started backing up against the wall, some of them getting dizzy because of the high energy!

Oh, about the symbol being drawn in the air by the bobber. What was it? I wondered the same thing and only recently got an explanation I don't fully understand. At the Southwest Dowsing Conference in Flagstaff, Arizona, I gave a presentation where the energy was raised by this method. A gentleman came up to me and said, "I know what that symbol is. It's the symbol I've found in crop circles." That night he presented an interesting slide show on crop circles containing various designs. One of them was the one my bobber had been drawing. This reinforced the belief that I was working with a force more intelligent than I.

OK, we have demonstrated that we can get the attention of an audience. What other benefit does this have? The benefits of raising the energy are probably unlimited, but in many cases, determining whether the energy has been raised will not be provable. After raising the energy, we can expect people to have positive changes in behavior. And, if the expected positive change occurs after we have raised the energy, perhaps that would indicate we had something to do with it.

One of my friends called yesterday and was depressed.

"I don't like Januarys," she said. "They're gloomy. It's this way every year."

Today she called back and in a very cheerful voice asked, "Did you do something to me yesterday? My outlook on life has changed. I feel happy!"

All I did was change the energy within her energy field. The way this was done was to just ask to raise the energy in her body and home to the highest appropriate level for her best good, while using either the pendulum or bobber.

My best success to this date was at the Canadian Health Show in Toronto. There were 600 seats in the auditorium and they were all filled, with many people standing around the walls. For some reason, the promoters had invited me to be one of the panel speakers at the event. Invitations like this continue to amaze me, as I show up in faded jeans, boots, and either a black Stetson hat or headband. I seldom have notes, and if so, don't read them. Never know what I'm going to say and when finished, don't remember much of what I said. Seems like something just takes over and the people usually like what happened.

On this particular day, the panel speakers were seated behind a table on the stage, with a microphone. It came my turn to speak. Being the only speaker without letters after my name, there was no reason to try to impress anyone.

I just said, "Watermelon is the biggest word I know, so this is going to be simple. Let's raise some energy." I took the bobber in hand, while still telling stories, and it drew the usual diagram in the air and began a strong clockwise spin. In a few minutes,

I asked, "How many of you felt an energy shift?" Most hands went up. I then asked, "How many of you folks have any pain or discomfort?" Perhaps 400 hands went up. I told them that we would see if we could get rid of the pain in their bodies. I asked to scramble the frequency of the pain and adjust it to their ideal body frequency. The bobber swung in a counterclockwise manner for several minutes.

Again the audience was asked, "How many of you have felt a decrease in the amount of pain in your body? About 250 hands went up. For the remainder of the weekend people came by our booth just to tell us that they didn't hurt anymore. It was a good day.

Using Energy to Change the Future

Bill was always talking about energy; one night he called and made this statement: "We can take the energy from a past event and send it into the future to change a future event."

This was interesting. We needed to test it. An opportunity was on the way. One of my friends in another state was fond of bears. He and his friends thought it terrible that people would chase them with dogs and shoot them. They had a plan to discourage this activity. They would go into the woods the day before hunting season, tie a bear hide to a rope and drag it through the mountains, thereby leaving a false trail and confusing the dogs. It was a good plan, but it had a serious flaw. Bear hunters were likely to take a dim view of such activities and they carried guns. To complicate matters, the day before hunting season this man's friends found other less dangerous things to do.

He still felt strongly about this and called for advice. Let me say here that I have been a hunter and still have many friends who are. I had just reached a point where I choose not to kill anything unless necessary. I had nothing against the bear hunters. I just needed someone to experiment with. Since my friend had asked for help and the bear hunters had not, they were qualified for the experiment.

My advice to him was, "Change your attitude and go into the woods as a hiker. If you meet the bear hunters, be nice to them and just stay close enough to observe them. Call me when it's over."

Picking up my pendulum, I asked, "Is there a past event from which to draw energy appropriate for this situation?" "Yes."

"What is the event?" I asked.

The information came as a strong thought: "The California earthquake." My mind questioned, "There were many energies at such a time. Which one should be used?"

Again the answer came, "Confusion." Again my mind questioned, "Are you telling me we can take the confusion from the earthquake and place it in the camp of the bear hunters?"

"Yes"

"OK, how do I do it?" I wondered.

"Just ask," came the response.

"OK, please do it now." The pendulum swung rapidly for a few minutes and stopped, leaving me wondering if anything had happened. Three days later my friend called excitedly to report the results and said, "They didn't get any sleep, fought among themselves, lost the dogs, and drove their truck into the lake twice."

Giving this more serious thought, I realized I didn't even know which earthquake had been used. I asked, "Does one need to have knowledge of the past event being used?"

"No."

"Does there even have to be a past event?" I questioned.

"No," came the reply again.

"Am I to understand that an energy can be created or formed simply by asking and by intent?"

"Yes."

This opened up countless possibilities. More experiments were in order. The following story relates one.

Someone asked me to lay some block for him on a difficult job no one else wanted, and I sure didn't want it. But the person couldn't find anyone else to do it and I like to help people.

"This will be expensive," I said, "due to the bad working conditions."

The homeowner replied, "It has to be done and no one else is available."

After agreeing to do the job, I simply asked for the most appropriate energy to be placed around me, my helper, and the job site, allowing me to work efficiently and cheerfully. The job was completed in record time with a good profit and a saving of several hundred dollars for the homeowner. Since then, the same principle has been used hundreds of times with beneficial results.

Let me give a few examples. One day a friend called, telling me about a dentist appointment in about an hour. Previous visits to this dentist had left much to be desired. The dentist didn't communicate well and visits were painful ordeals.

My friend was really dreading the appointment that day, as it involved some major dental work. I told her to go on anyway and not worry about it. This was hardly any comfort to her but she had little choice. Next day, she called and was excited to report that the visit went extremely well. The dentist was nice to her and there was no pain.

All I did was ask to create the most appropriate energy around Jeannie, the dentist, the dental assistant, and the office and for the dentist to work quickly, skillfully, and painlessly. The dowsing device will move in a clockwise manner when doing this.

The previous story of the bear hunters has been told so many times that it's threadbare. Eileen was in my class, listening to the story, and decided to use the principles to solve a similar problem. Please remember that these techniques can be used to solve otherwise *unsolvable* problems with elected officials. Do not underestimate the power of this technique; after all, I didn't invent it, it was a gift of the spirit world. Here's Eileen.

Eileen's Story

I remember Raymon telling how he sent the vibration of the energy of confusion to an area where hunters were after big game—bear I think—with the desire to prevent any harm coming to the animals, causing the hunters to leave the area. The story impressed me very much, for a number of reasons. It's a great use of mind in that it can be done without causing any harm to anyone. I always stress that in energy work; that it cause no harm. I learned the hard way that if I don't intend that, it leaves a lot of loose ends I haven't considered that could possibly result in harm coming to someone. For years, we've had problems with hunters in the woods behind our house. Hunters weren't supposed to be there at all according to the State law, but the local authorities didn't pay much mind to it because many of the local policemen liked to use it as a private hunting ground. Last year, a group of us neighbors got together and went to town meetings to request a moratorium on the hunting, which was dangerously close to many residences.

I asked for help and visualized a successful resolution to the problem. Well, there was a partial success to that effort. The town agreed to limit the hunting to a small area of the woods (with no assurance that the restricted area would ever be patrolled, which meant in effect that there was really no restriction on hunting). So, I borrowed Raymon's method of projecting the energy vibration of confusion, requesting and intending that the energy prevent all hunters from harming or killing any animal in these particular woods, causing no harm to anyone. I did this several times. For the first time, in the 30-odd years I've lived here, all hunting has now been banned. Nobody in an official capacity is saying why. I'd like to think that the work I did had something to do with the total ban. It is my belief that this type of work has many applications for us on this planet, and I'm so happy to have learned about it. Thank you, Raymon.

Eileen Lilly

Dealing with Negativity

Raising the energy is a most beneficial act, but it isn't the entire story. In order to raise the energy effectively, it is necessary to have a person or area cleared of negativity. One might ask, what type of negativity? Let us explore the question in detail.

Any time I am asked to work with a person or to improve conditions in a home or business or any other area, there are specific questions to be addressed. For example, when asked to improve conditions in a home, I would ask a series of questions of the pendulum in the following order:

1. Are there any negative entities possessing this house or property? How many?

   It is probably not necessary to know how many. It just seems that the more information we have, the more efficient we are. I just always ask this question. You would get either a yes or no to the question of the property being possessed. If the answer is yes, then you can ask how many and watch to see where the pendulum swings on the chart. The chart referred to is the one in Walt Wood's manual, *Letter to Robin*, and is located in the back of this book.

2. Are there any negative entities present in this house or property? How many?

   Many times a person or property will have negative entities present but not actually possessing the person or property. They may be just present in the energy field of the person. Once it is determined that negative entities are present, the next step is to communicate with your Spirit Guide, Guardian Angel, or Spirit Helper—pick the one you like. Ask them to take the negative entities to the other side where they will be given the appropriate treatment and sent on to the proper realm. We are making no judgments as to where this is.

My pendulum will move in the "yes" position until they are removed and then it will swing to the "no" position. Your pendulum may swing in a different manner. Don't worry about it—what is important is the results you get.

3. Are there any negative "energetic patterns" adversely affecting the property? If yes, ask them to be neutralized.

"Energetic patterns" is a name picked to identify the energy left by some negative event of the past. An example of this would be the energy left on a battlefield where people have suffered and died.

4. Are there any hexes or curses of any type adversely affecting this home or property? How many?

Count them the same as before and ask to have them removed. A person does not need a Ph.D. in witchcraft in order to put a curse on someone or their home. A curse is an extreme negative thought form that can be created by most anyone, even the person themselves.

5. Are there any non-beneficial thought forms present which are adversely affecting this house or property?

If so, all things being energy and changeable, transform them into their opposite.

6. Are there any poltergeists located in, or adversely affecting, this house or property?

If so, a different term is called for. The term is "spirit doctors." Ask the spirit doctors to take them to another dimension and lock them up so they can never return to Earth. Any time objects are disappearing from a home, it is safe to assume that a poltergeist may be present. In one instance, a policeman was losing his equipment; it was just disappearing from his home. When the four poltergeists were removed, the equipment started to reappear.

7. What is the percentage of available life force on this property?

This is measured in percentages, 100 percent being ideal. (Note: You can measure the life force, both before and after you work. As the various negative elements are removed, measure the life force. You will notice that each time a correction is made, the life force will improve.)

8. What is the energy level on this property?

This is measured in increments of one thousand. This number has been continually rising for the past five years. In September 1998 the ideal energy level was about 8,000; at this writing it is more like 23,000.

9. What is the "love level" in this house?

This indicates the level of compatibility and love among those living in the house. It is measured by percentage and ideally is 100 percent. If you find the love level to be below zero, you know the folks have problems. If invited for dinner, look for bullet holes in the walls, and watch for a spider in your dumplings.

Again, as the negative elements are removed, the love level will in most cases improve.

There are many other things to look for that can and do affect the energy of a person or place. Those listed are the most common problems and, usually, removing them will greatly improve living conditions in a home or business.

To date, Larry Huszczo and I have more than 100 things to look for when clearing people or places. To explain all of this takes two days of class time. This is why only the more common ones are listed here.

11 Exorcism

Even though various titles have been given to chapters, the information all blends together. In order to effectively make lasting improvements, the list of questions in the previous chapter needs to be addressed. Let's start with negative entities possessing the house or property. What are they and where do they come from? Most of the ones I have found I believe to be the spirits of someone who once lived on earth. However, I make no claims to be an expert concerning these things. The point is, there are things that adversely affect people and property. When these things are removed, conditions improve. Let me give some stories to help you understand this.

One morning I received a call from a friend concerning her son who had been arrested for drunk driving. She asked if I could do something to get him out of trouble.

My answer was, "No, I think drunk drivers should be put in jail before they kill some innocent family."

As we continued to talk, I really felt sorry for her. He was her son and she loved him. Maybe I could be a bit more diplomatic.

"Tell me," I asked, "Has he ever been knocked unconscious?"

"Yes, a few years ago," she answered.

"Did his behavior change?" I asked.

"Immediately and drastically," she replied.

"OK. I think I know what the problem is," I told her. "Let me see what I can do about it."

Four days later I saw her and she was just beaming with happiness. "He has changed! He's so much better!" she exclaimed.

Two weeks later I spoke with her husband and this is what he had to say, "I don't know what you did to that boy, but he hasn't been the same since you worked on him."

What did I do? I de-possessed him. How did I know he was possessed? I asked by use of the dowsing system, with the aid of a pendulum described in the last chapter. How did I know what to ask? Well, this is one of the benefits of learning to use your mind.

There seem to be conditions that are conducive to a person becoming possessed. These conditions include unconsciousness, a state of shock, and the influence of drugs or alcohol.

Another case was a call I got one day from someone I had never met. The conversation went something like this.

"There is something wrong with my husband. He isn't the same any more. He is trying to sell cars, but sold only one last month. He is depressed, won't talk much, and just wants to come home and drink beer. We don't even have grocery money!"

While she was talking, I was using my pendulum to check on him. It didn't take long to find the problem.

"Don't tell him you talked to me. Wait three days and call me again," I told her.

The reason I didn't want him to know she had talked to me was to remove the power of suggestion. If we can influence the behavior of a person without their knowledge, then we know power of suggestion played no part in it.

After three days she called and excitedly exclaimed, "Whatever you are doing, please keep it up! He came home a few hours after you and I talked and he was his old self. He has sold three cars since then and doesn't drink anymore."

Again, this was a simple case of de-possession. Let's see if we can determine what had taken place in these two cases.

It is recorded in the Bible that King Solomon said something like, "As a man thinks in his heart, so he is." If King Solomon didn't say something like that, he certainly should have. This is another way of saying you will attract the people, circumstances, and events to fulfill whatever you truly believe in your heart. This statement will also be appropriate to use later.

Bear with me for a few moments. When someone dies, his or her body is buried, burned, or disposed of in some way. But what happens to their spirit? Would it depend upon their belief system? If they had the belief they would be carried away by a flock of angels, maybe they were right. If they believed there would be angels coming to get them riding six white horses, maybe they were right. If they believed they would take a walk to the "happy hunting ground," maybe they were right. If they believed they were terrible and the devil was coming for them to take them to hell, maybe they were right.

But what would happen if they didn't believe there was anywhere to go? Or what if they had been victims of hellfire and damnation sermons and knew they weren't good enough for heaven and afraid of hell? Where do their spirits go?

I realize the good people I attended church with will be shocked at such questions, but experience has given me reason for asking.

Perhaps their spirits stay at the place where they were separated from the body, which in many cases would be the hospital. I have found numerous spirits in churches. It seems they are there because it offers security. Other places they may be found are in the homes where they lived. This is especially true if they were strongly attached to their possessions. I am greatly inclined to believe that the spirits of alcoholics are attracted to bars.

Let's return to the case of the young man who was driving drunk. What had happened to him? This is the way I put it together. The main thing that changes when people die is they no longer have physical bodies. It seems they retain many of their habits but have no body to fulfill these desires. An alcoholic will want a drink, but has no body with which to drink. A most frustrating condition, I would imagine. There were two spirits of alcoholics in the emergency room of the hospital where this young man lay unconscious. His energy field was weak and they were able to move in and take over, thus giving them a body to drink with. This also affected his personality. Once they were removed, their influence upon him was also removed, allowing him to be in control of himself. A similar situation existed with the other example I gave of the car salesman.

Once upon a time I used to chase ghosts out of houses. This was quite exciting at times, but was also quite time consuming, as I had to go to the house and perform the exorcism.

On one occasion, I was asked to visit someone who had a stomach condition that had defied medical treatment. The person also had a frozen shoulder, preventing her arm from being lifted more than a few inches. This condition had persisted for many months with no improvement. Upon arriving at the house, I asked the lady to open the window, although it was a cold day. I then loaded my old bee smoker with cedar shavings and set them on fire. Walking to the end of the hall, I turned right, walked into the bedroom and opened the closet door. Pumping the billows of the bee smoker a few times produced a big cloud of smoke. Then I proceeded to puff the smoke into the closet. A strange thing happened. It puffed back at me. This was contrary to the nature of smoke and assured me that I had found the problem. Taking my eagle feather and letting out a high pitched scream, I demanded that all evil spirits and associates "get the hell out!" When I came back to where the lady was waiting by the open window, she informed me, "Something cold came down the hall and went out the window."

"That is why I asked you to leave the window open," I told her. "Now, let's see if we can fix your shoulder."

I did some simple energy work and much to her surprise, her arm went up to about the level of her shoulder.

"Come visit me in a couple of days and we will finish the job," I stated.

She and her husband arrived two days later at my house and after a small amount of energy work on her shoulder, she could put her arm over her head. Within two weeks the stomach problem had cleared up.

Looking back, it seems there was an entity in the house that was draining her energy. This happened back in my early days of doing energy work. At the time, I was not knowledgeable enough to recognize many of the problems I know about today. Back then, I simply did things with brute strength and determination. Now, after having learned more, I simply send a representative who is my Spirit Guide. Spirit Guides will be discussed in the next chapter.

The following two letters were received as this chapter was being written. The first letter refers to an experience a few years ago. The second one happened more recently. My work was done in response to a request to "do something" about the problem described in the letters written by Jane, Tony's wife. (Names have been changed for privacy.)

This occurrence was about three to four years ago:

> Tony had been drinking more than usual and was making our
> lives simply unbearable. He was spending a lot of time at the bar

in town, and seemed to be losing all focus on his family and life in general. Somewhere along the way, I had talked with Elizabeth, Tony's mother, about how bad things were getting and that I didn't know how much longer I was going to be able to hang in there with Tony. Although he and I have always been very close, there does come a time when you say, "Enough is enough!"

I woke up one night and glanced toward our bedroom wall. The moonlight was shining in through the window, not brightly, but making it easy to make out shapes and silhouettes. The light was reflecting off of the bathroom door. Tony was lying beside me in bed, sound asleep, between the door and me. All of a sudden I noticed a kind of fog coming up from him. It glowed a bit in the moonlight. As it rose, this fog took the shape of a skeleton. It was still transparent and had only a vague outline, but it definitely was in the form of a human skeleton. I am sure that most women having just witnessed a foggy skeleton rising from their husband's body in the middle of the night would have gone running for the hills . . . but I simply felt at peace and went back to sleep. I still remember it as if it happened yesterday, however. It was not a dream. My eyes were fully open and I was fully conscious at the time.

Tony awoke the next morning, a seemingly changed man. He was his "old self." I told him that I thought he should go see a therapist who dealt with addictions. In the past, every time I mentioned this, it was met with hostility. This time, however, he agreed. He picked up the phone and made an appointment, there on the spot. He met with a therapist that afternoon. When he came home, I asked how things went and he replied, "Oh, they went fine." I then inquired when his next appointment was and he looked me right in the eye and said, "You know, I don't really think I need help with this." I thought, "Here we go again. He'll be back drinking in no time and going on being nasty." But he was right. He didn't need help with it. He stopped drinking completely for a whole year, not a drop of alcohol the entire year. He now drinks a beer every now and again, and even drinks too much at times, though this is now a rare occurrence. He certainly doesn't have the drinking problem he had back then, and to this day he remains the warm and caring person that I knew him to be, not the angry man he had turned into for a while.

Oh, by the way, I didn't find out that you had worked on Tony until several days after I saw the apparition. Elizabeth had called to find out how things were going and I told her how much better things were. She then told me she had you work on Tony. We pinpointed that her conversation with you happened on the same evening that I saw the apparition coming from Tony in our bedroom.

Here is the second letter:

It started off with the Fresno Police Department sending Elizabeth a letter stating that they wanted us to evict the tenants of a house owned by Elizabeth, Tony's mother, because the tenants were suspected drug dealers and a real nuisance to the entire neighborhood. After several contacts by both mail and phone, the tenants were persuaded to move out, without too much resistance. The first time Tony and I stepped foot inside, we had combined feelings of disgust and fear. The house was filthy. It appeared to not have been cleaned for years. Every inch of every wall in the entire house was covered in some sort of black sooty substance. The carpets were filthy. The walls had holes in them and several windows were broken and/or missing completely. The yards were filled with garbage strewn about and the neighborhood was as scary as the house itself. From the minute we arrived, the noise was so loud it was hard to concentrate. There were barking dogs everywhere. Two kids ran into the yard and immediately started taking what they wanted and generally being a nuisance. There was a constant yelling back and forth among adults who were either yelling from yard to yard, or to others as they walked by. Some of the yelling was friendly and some was not. All in all, the neighborhood was simply *loud* with much commotion at all times.

For the first five or so days that we did repair work to the house, we had to work through the noise of the neighborhood and contend with nightly break-ins. The first day Tony replaced two windows. When we returned the next morning, one was broken out and the tools that we had left inside the house were gone. Tony repaired the window. We worked and went home. The second day the same thing. There was garbage thrown all over inside the house. We cleaned it up, worked some more, and went home.

Both Tony and I came down with severe flu-like symptoms about this time and so, from then on, not only were we working in a bad environment, we both felt terrible.

The next day we returned to find the back door kicked open and a mess inside, again. By this time we weren't leaving anything but odds and ends, and everything down to a pencil would be stolen when we returned. Keep in mind that this entire time the neighborhood was in an uproar, with barking dogs, yelling neighbors, and kids who would come in and out of the house while we were trying to repair it. We went about our work and Tony installed a dead bolt in the door that had been kicked open the night before. We locked everything up tight and went to get lunch.

An hour later we returned to find this same door kicked in with such force that the framework around it had been splintered. We immediately went inside to find the back window open with footprints in the mud outside. We think that the perpetrators were inside when we came back from lunch and made their escape through the back. This was the last straw. We phoned the police, who never came, because crime is so prevalent in the area, I guess it didn't warrant a report.

Unbeknownst to us, Elizabeth had called you to work on both the house and us that evening. You know the details on your end. We didn't go back the next day because we simply didn't want to face whatever was there. Remember, we did not know that you had worked on anything. That night when we went to bed, I remember asking Tony how he felt, as we were both terribly sick. He thought a moment and said, "You know, I feel fine." He took a deep breath in through his nose. "I really do feel fine." I said, "Me too. I feel absolutely well."

The next day Tony went to the house first. He said that when he opened the door, it had a calm, quiet feeling. He took note of it and started about his work. When I arrived, I got out of the car to a *very* quiet neighborhood. I could see the dogs in the neighbors' yards, but they were silent. There was absolutely no barking in the entire neighborhood that is just filled with dogs. No kids swarmed out to bother us in our work. There was no yelling. In fact, I didn't see a living soul. I went into the house and everything was neat and tidy, just the way we had left it. My initial apprehension left. Nothing was broken, stolen, or destroyed. I felt much safer than I had previously felt at this house. We set about our work.

A few hours had gone by when Elizabeth called me on my cell phone and asked how everything was at the house. I told her what we had found and that Tony and I were both feeling well, so hopefully, we could hurry up and get things repaired and be out of there. I told her about the neighborhood being unusually quiet and that no kids had come over to pester us. This was before she told us that you had worked on the house. She then told me that you had worked on both the house and us.

From that morning forward, the neighborhood has been quiet; no dogs barking, no break-ins, nothing stolen, nothing destroyed, and Tony and I are still well. I cannot think of one adverse occurrence happening after you worked on the house. We spent approximately six more days working there after you worked on the place and each day we were met with quiet and calmness. We finished all of the remodeling work and now it is a nice little house, nothing like the mess we first walked into.

This was the result of combined exorcism, energy clearing, and energy raising—all with the help of my Spirit Helpers.

Many times there are good people we would not normally suspect who have entities possessing them. For example, Sonya called one day and asked me to check on a friend who had a strong urge to jump in front of moving cars. This lady was a member of a fundamental religious group known to bounce off the walls, but jumping in front of cars was not generally practiced. When I inquired into the matter, it was obvious the lady was possessed by an entity that caused her to have suicidal tendencies. I suspect this occurred during an emotional religious service in which she had lost control of her body and mind. An evil spirit was lurking in the shadows waiting to pounce on an unsuspecting victim who believed she was giving her heart to Jesus. The entity was removed and a call was received from Sonya a week later stating that the woman had experienced a change of heart. Jumping in front of cars had lost its appeal.

I never met this lady and she has no idea what happened or that I even exist. It was just another random act of kindness upon a misguided soul.

And what if all this is just a coincidence? Well, that's what it's about, making coincidences happen.

12 Spirit Helpers

On reading the previous chapters, one might assume that I did the work alone. This is not true. Much, if not all, of the work is done by combined efforts of the spirit world and myself. Many of the things written here are unprovable but are told the way I believe them to be.

When I was still employing the bee smoker and eagle feather method, I was asked to clear a house. This house had a room that was colder than the rest of the house. Mildew would form on items stored in the room. April, who was about eight years old, accompanied me on this trip. I thought maybe she might need to know how to chase ghosts sometime in her life and this would be good experience. She held the eagle feather while I started the fire in the bee smoker and I asked the homeowner to open the kitchen window. I then started through the house puffing smoke everywhere and all at once the energy changed in the house. The homeowner was real excited and saying something about a scream coming through the house and going out the window. The temperature normalized in the room and no mildew formed there again. For April, this was no big deal. She was more interested in going to get some ice cream.

As time went by, I met Eugene Maurey, who taught me how to do this work with much less wear and tear on myself. It is no longer necessary to physically go to the house to perform this work. I simply send a representative.

Let's take the example of the house in Fresno written about in the last chapter. Using my pendulum to check on this house, I found it to be possessed with 18 negative entities or evil spirits. I asked my Spirit Helper if he was willing and able to remove them and received a "yes." I then requested him to go to the house, get all the negative entities there, take them kicking, screaming and dragging their heels to the "other side," where they would be given the appropriate treatment and go on to wherever they were supposed to go.

Now is a good time to address an issue that comes up from time to time. There are certain good souls among my friends who choose not to believe in what I refer to as negative entities. I really don't blame them. I would rather not believe in them either. Truth is, I would rather not believe that the following elements of our society exist: child molesters, rapists, serial killers, starvation, drugs, corrupt politicians, and several others. But the fact that I choose not to believe in them does not make them go away, nor does it make them less of a threat to humanity. Not accepting the existence of gravity does not prevent us from falling off a cliff.

My question to these friends is this: "If the negative entities do not exist, then why do conditions improve when they are removed?"

Another question: "Why do you call me to remove them from your homes and workplaces when you don't believe in them?" That's OK, you and I have worked out a satisfactory agreement. You continue to hold on to your beliefs that negative entities do not exist and you can pay me to get rid of them. I appreciate your business.

This is the general procedure for all exorcisms that I do. All I do is make the request. My Spirit Helper does the work. One may ask, "Why does the spirit world pay any attention to my request?" I believe we must "pay our dues." The spirit world has little interest in helping those who will not help themselves. Neither will abilities be provided for an extended time to those who will misuse or do not use them.

Since some of my teachers and friends have been Native Americans, I am often asked, "What have you learned from the Indians?" My answer in one word is, "Respect!"

These Native people lived here for thousands of years without harming the earth. The people from Europe, Asia, and Africa have been here fewer than 400 years and the top soil is eroded, trees are gone, water is poisoned, and the air is polluted.

Since all that we are and all we have comes from the Earth, the way the Earth has been treated is not only disrespectful, it is suicidal. It is my opinion that lack of respect is the basic cause of all the ills of humanity. If people had respect for the Creator, creation, each other, and themselves, we could eliminate war, crime, hunger, pollution, and most, if not all, of the social diseases.

One day on a small construction project, my very rough crew and I were eating lunch in the shade of a large oak tree. At times I feel moved to deliver a sermon and this was one of those times. Getting their attention, I announced, "Gentlemen, may I direct your attention to this oak tree. It has been here for well over a hundred years. During this time it has provided shade as we are enjoying now, acorns for the squirrels, a home for the birds to nest in, leaves to produce oxygen for us to breathe, roots to prevent erosion of the soil, and perhaps many other things of which we are unaware. In every way considered, this tree has been an asset to the earth and all associated with it. In no way has it been harmful to anything. That's a hell of a lot more than can be said of most people."

Jesus once taught what is known as the "parable of the talents." The moral to the story was to use whatever abilities or resources we have and they will be increased. The reverse being that if we do not use what we have, it will be taken away. Summed up it goes like this: "Use it or lose it."

When I first started doing healing work, I only knew one simple technique, so I used it. Then I learned more, and used them. This continues to this day. I tried to do things to help those who needed help and were willing to help themselves. Perhaps for this reason the spirit world responds to my request.

Once while driving through Tennessee, a number of crosses on the side of the road caught my attention. These crosses had been placed there in memory of the ones killed in car accidents. I could feel there were some spirits still there on the side of the road. I asked my Spirit Helpers or Guides if they thought it appropriate to assist these spirits, who were stuck here, to cross over to the other side. They agreed that it needed to be done.

I asked, "Then why don't you do it?"

The reply came back, "We're waiting for you."

This confused me and I asked, "Do you mean to tell me that you can't take these earthbound spirits on into the spirit world?"

"This is your job," they answered. "You see, we are of the spirit world and you are of the physical world. There are things we can do that you can't and there are things you can do that we can't. We need to work together."

With that information still churning in my mind, I asked the spirits by the side of the road if they were ready to go to the other side. They replied that they were and I led them down the path to the stairs leading to the Tunnel of Light. Up the stairs they went and into the tunnel and were gone.

Let's look at a few more cases. A few months ago a couple of my friends who had recently moved into a different house were visiting me. These were both sensitive people and informed me that they suspected that a ghost haunted their house. I informed them that it was not one, but three ghosts. They asked if I would come and remove them.

"No need to. Let's do it now." I said.

Within less that a minute the ghosts were gone and I asked my friends to give me some feedback. About a month later they told me that there were no further feelings of ghosts in the house.

All I did was ask my Spirit Guide to take them to the other side, get them the appropriate treatment, and send them on to where they were supposed to go.

While doing some stone work on an old house built in the 1840's, Mark, the owner, related a story about the previous owner, Glen, who had passed away.

He said, "Folks in the neighborhood believe Glen is still around. Someone saw him up on the hill recently but he disappeared. Would you check and see if he is still here?"

I "tuned in" to Glen and he was indeed still on the property. He had cared a lot for his farm and was concerned that no one else would care for it in the same manner. However, Mark had taken excellent care of the place and was making additional improvements. I assured Mark that Glen was pleased with the way he was running the farm and he was ready to move on.

"Would you assist him in crossing over?" he asked.

"Well, sometimes these things get emotional. Let me wait until tonight," I replied.

It occurred to me that an old house may also have collected some other spirits, and sure enough, there were nine more. These nine spirits were ready to leave but didn't seem to know how or where to go. There was a smaller building at the back of the house and Mark described it as the slave quarters. Following a hunch, I found the spirits of eight slaves in the building. When I asked if they were ready to cross over, they said, "No, we're waiting for something." I never gave much thought to this and went on with my work.

The next day Mark asked if I had assisted Glen in crossing over.

"No," I answered, "I forgot about it."

"Will you do it now?" he insisted.

Laying down my trowel, I reached in my pocket for the pendulum. Again I addressed the nine spirits and Glen, "Are you ready to cross over to another realm of the spirit world?"

The answer was, "Yes."

Then addressing the spirits of the slaves, I asked the same question.

The reply came back, "No, we're waiting for something."

"What are you waiting for?" I wanted to know.

Their answer surprised me, "Freedom."

"But don't you know that you were freed almost 140 years ago?" I questioned.

"No, we're still waiting," came the reply.

This caused me to think of things differently. Their spirits still existed in the same time as when they died.

"If I were to tell you that you were freed at the end of the Civil War, would you believe me?"

Again the answer came, "No, we wouldn't believe you."

I then addressed my Spirit Helper, whom I refer to as Grandfather because I believe that is who he is. "Grandfather, will you please tell these slaves that they have been free a long time and it is time to go now?"

"They won't believe me either," he said.

"Do you know of anyone who could talk to them whom they would believe?" I asked.

Let me say here that this was a mental conversation with pictures of the events floating through my mind.

It appeared that Grandfather went somewhere in the spirit world and found an old Black preacher and sent him to speak with the spirits of the slaves. In a few moments, all eight of them came and were ready to leave. I mentally explained to them where we were going and asked them to follow me down the path to the steps. They climbed the steps and walked into the Tunnel of Light. Glen had waited until the others had gone, then he thanked me and stepped into the tunnel and was gone.

Evelyn Rattray of British Columbia has been mentioned earlier and I would like to relate another story concerning her.

Evelyn was speaking at the Power of Thought Conference in Fort St. John, British Columbia, and I was in the audience. She told of a recent visit to eastern Canada where she encountered some energy that bothered her. It seems there was a military plane that crashed several years ago and killed all those on the plane. This incident happened near the place she was visiting. Being a most sensitive person, Evelyn had felt the energy of these spirits and the feeling was disturbing to her. She could "see" the soldiers lying in the plane, piled on top of each other. The next day we were talking and she told me the same story again. This got my attention and I wondered why she was repeating the story to me. Without telling her what I was doing or thinking, I tuned in to the soldiers and asked them if they were ready to cross over. They were. I then asked if they knew how. They didn't.

"If I were to show you how to go to another realm of the spirit world, would you follow me?" I asked. They would.

Just as in the other stories, I led them down the path, but something happened. They got in a column of four abreast just like marching in the Army, and marched. When we got to the stairs, the commanding officer stood at attention at the bottom while the soldiers double timed up the stairs. The officer walked up the stairs, turned, and saluted me, then stepped into the tunnel.

"Will you look at them again and tell me what you see?" I inquired of Evelyn.

"They're gone!" she exclaimed. "But there is a lot of white light where they were, and everything feels much lighter."

On the same trip to Canada, I had the privilege of working with a Canadian Mountie. This Mountie worked on an Indian Reserve that had a high rate of abuse—alcohol, drug, sexual, and most any other kind. I was asked to do something about this situation. This project was considerably larger than any I had tackled previously, but if we do nothing, nothing will happen. So I did something.

The first thing to do was determine how many negative entities possessed the people and the land and clear them. Next was to determine how many were just "hanging around" and clear them also. The way this was done was to ask Grandfather if he was willing and able to do the job. The answer was "yes." My request was made in the manner stated earlier to take them to the other side. Then a check was made for poltergeists, and the spirit doctors were asked to take them to their proper place where they could never return or do any harm.

The next thing I inquired about was "curses on the land." I simply asked to neutralize them. I suppose curses are just another form of energy. If this is true, then we should be able to transform them into blessings.

A check was then made for noxious energy rays and the non-beneficial frequencies were removed from them and changed into something beneficial. (Noxious energy rays come up from the Earth and strongly affect people in a negative manner. They will usually be located under a bed, chair, or a place where a person spends a lot of time. I have even found them coming up through a toilet seat. It seems in many cases that noxious energy rays and evil spirits go hand in hand. I believe the noxious energy rays provide an atmosphere to attract evil spirits. Once, a friend asked me to check the office where she worked because the people in the office were grouchy and ill. She drew a sketch of the office, and in going over it with my pendulum, I found four noxious energy rays. She noticed each place I marked on the sketch was a place where someone's chair was located. I removed the noxious energy rays and asked for some feedback, but asked her to tell no one of our work. Next day, the people were excitedly asking, "What is going on here? We feel so much better!")

The next question concerned the Indian Reserve: "Are there any non-beneficial thought forms and/or non-beneficial energies affecting the people or land?" There were and I asked that they be transformed into their opposites. Sometimes we may not know exactly what to ask for and to transform anything which is non-beneficial into its opposite seems the most appropriate thing to do. While the transformation was being made, the pendulum swung in a clockwise manner.

Here is an example of clearing energy that I use in class: "If you come home and find water running under your door, go inside and look for the tub running over, then turn it off. It does little good to get a mop and bucket until you turn the water off."

So it is with clearing a person or property. We must eliminate the negative influences before effective positive changes can be made. This is what has been described in the past several paragraphs. It was now time to change the life force and energy.

The only definition I have for "life force" is: "It's what puts the sparkle in your eye." Life force is measured by percentage on the chart mentioned earlier. The goal was to raise the life force to 100 percent. Once that had been done, the next step was to raise the "energy level"; then the "love level" and/or "cooperation level" was raised. The work was now completed. All we had to do was wait and see what happened.

A week later I spoke with a very surprised Mountie. Instead of the usual numerous calls coming into the office for violent offenses, there were only two calls the entire week. One concerned a drunken person and the other was a complaint of a loud party. I received a call about five weeks later stating that conditions were still favorable. I was told, "You haven't solved all the problems, but things are sure better than they were."

While I was teaching a class at the Ozark Research Institute in Arkansas, someone in the class made a strange request. This was a friend of mine named Robert who told of a school where cries for help were heard by the custodians late at night. This seemed to be children crying and had gone on for years, but no source of the cries was ever found.

Robert had researched the matter and found that more than 60 years ago the school caught fire and several children were killed. He asked me if I could do anything about it.

I stopped the class and tuned in to the children and led them down the path, up the stairs, and into the Tunnel of Light. It was a very emotional experience for the entire class, so emotional that I had to walk out of the classroom. A year or so later Robert informed me that no cries had been heard since.

Much thought has been given to incidences such as these. It seems that if we are privileged to live on this Earth, we should do something to make conditions better. I have often wondered if freeing an Earth-bound spirit might be the most benevolent act one could perform.

In my classes people learn how to reach a realm of the spirit world and meet their Spirit Guides. Some recognize these spirits with names, some with descriptions, and some just take it for granted that they are there. It seems the description of one's

Spirit Guides are relative to a person's religion or belief system. For instance, a deeply religious person may perceive angels while one less religious may have a relative of the past. Most of those attending my class have a tendency to get Native Americans as guides. It may be because of the atmosphere in which the class is presented. I use a drumbeat to assist in inviting the spirits.

In all honesty, not everyone gets a Spirit Guide in these sessions. There is no way I know of to make them appear or cause the student to perceive them. However, this doesn't seem to be an obstacle in getting the job done. It seems that all we need to do is ask with intent—if you have paid your dues.

13 Low-Class Spooks and Other Junk

April, Nancy, and I get along well, but one day we started getting very irritable with each other. It was so bad that I was pacing the floor while Nancy was fixing lunch. I suggested that maybe it was some "messed up" energy affecting us. Nancy asked if I could do something about it. I was desperate enough to try anything, just didn't know what to try. After employing the pendulum and confirming that we weren't possessed, I began to look for other things. It was then the spirit world intervened and said, "Ask about non-beneficial frequencies."

Not having a clue as to what non-beneficial frequencies were, I asked and got a "yes."

My request then was, "Will you please eliminate them or transform them into something beneficial?"

The pendulum swung counterclockwise for a few minutes and stopped. Within five minutes a peaceful atmosphere had returned. This gave me something to think about. The attitude of my family had been changed in a matter of minutes and I didn't really know what had been done.

One point I would like to make here is that we do not need complete information to solve a problem. What we do need is a willingness to do something about it. If we do nothing, nothing will happen. If we do something, something will probably happen.

A short time later, on a construction job, my entire crew got angry with each other. This feeling of anger extended to the homeowner, truck driver, and me. After getting my wits together enough to realize what was happening, I stepped back out of the way and using my pendulum, checked on the presence of non-beneficial frequencies. They were present in abundance. Again, I simply asked to either have them removed or transformed into something beneficial. The pendulum then swung counterclockwise for a few minutes and stopped. This time it took about 15 minutes for things to change, but then everyone was happy. They were laughing and talking about what was wrong with them earlier.

This was a small investment of time and effort to achieve favorable working conditions.

It has been my experience that these non-beneficial frequencies affect men in different ways than they affect women. To sum it up, the presence of these things seems to make men angry and women tired. This is certainly not true in all cases, but seems true most of the time. In each instance I have asked my audience, "How many of the women here have noticed within the past two years that your husband or boyfriend becomes angry without a reason?" Most, if not all, women raise their hands.

I realize that some will say the time frame could be extended back for many more years and in some cases this is true. However, the point I wish to make is that we seem to be going through a time of energy changes upon the Earth, unlike any we have experienced before. I believe we can do something about it.

Low-Level Spooks

Another thing that affects people is something Bill Askin calls "mutated spooks" and Walt Woods calls "low-level entities." It seems at times when a person has a positive thought or desire to do something beneficial, these "low-level entities" are either activated or attracted.

Many times I will ask the audience, "How many of you have a really worthwhile project, but you keep getting blocked from carrying it out?" Upon checking the individual cases, most of them were affected by these low-level entities.

What are these things anyway? I'm not sure, but am reminded of a passage in the Bible that may possibly relate to them. The apostle Paul is reported in the King James version to have said something like this, "When I would do good, evil is present with me." Was he speaking of low-level entities? I don't know. What is important is to know how to get rid of them.

To create a rapid "spook be gone," just ask the power you work with to destroy them.

There is most always some well-meaning person in the audience who finds this method too harsh for their comfort. These good people suggest sending them to the Light. Maybe that's the reason their ghost bustin' doesn't work real well. In clearing negative entities and other spiritual trash, I adopt the mentality of a warlord.

This is a good time to give an opinion on something else. Too many times I've witnessed good people going through miserable situations, which appear to be no fault of their own. They are usually being drained emotionally and financially by a relative or an associate. This wouldn't be so bad if the good people could just pick up those who are in a bad situation, help them on their feet, and turn them loose. It seldom happens that way, but usually continues for years. Many would characterize this as karma, and that may be true. I suspect many times a person will receive as much of this type karma as they believe they deserve and are willing to tolerate. This is not to say that all problems will be changed by our refusal to accept them, but by golly, we can lighten the load!

Let me tell you a story about a dog and a cat. The dog was a large and fierce Doberman who loved to intimidate the cat, which was terrified of the dog. The dog would "put the evil eye" on the cat, causing it to become very nervous, with good reason. In a few moments the cat's nerve would cave in and away it would go toward the nearest tree with the dog in hot pursuit. This practice continued each time the cat would leave the barn to come to the house. One day the dog began his usual stalk on the cat. This presented a problem for the cat, as he was cornered with no available trees and nowhere to run. The dog kept getting closer and the cat was getting more nervous. When the dog's nose was inches from the cat, a dramatic shift took place. The cat lashed out and left four bloody claw marks across the dog's nose. Never again did the dog attempt to intimidate the cat. He had become converted.

I learned something that day. A lot of stuff happens to us because we put up with it.

Remember, *Keep on doin' what you're doin,' and you'll keep on gettin' what you're gettin'.* One definition of insanity has been, doing the same thing and expecting different results.

Curses

A few times I have found curses on people, even entire families. These have affected people in various ways, including sickness, poverty, and general bad luck. When the curses are removed, there is an overall improvement in the person. The following story is an example of this and is in the writer's own words. The names have been changed.

I was having major problems with my two teens—my boy Sam, 18, and girl Sarah, 15. My son had suffered many bouts of depression and having finished school, was totally lethargic, unable to motivate himself to call friends, go out anywhere, or search for work. He was couch bound with an attitude of apathy.

My daughter was filled with fear. She was able to attend school, but had many problems dealing with any projects that required her to address the class or approach any outside person—for example, bank tellers, checkout clerks, or anyone of that nature. Her teachers complained that she was quiet and never shared anything in class. She is a brilliant student and they wanted her to contribute.

I had a crisis with my son on a trip. Something of his was broken in the car and he turned violent, releasing his anger on his sister and me. I was desperate for help. I remembered an article written by Raymon Grace in the *Sedona Journal*. I called Raymon and he worked to adjust the energy in the children from his home. I was skeptical and desperate. It was the very day he made the adjustments that the children lightened up. They began to get along and things seemed much better. I wrote and told Raymon things were better, but I was with them daily so wasn't sure how much better. Raymon wrote back and said he had looked again and had found a curse on them; he'd worked to remove it.

It was the next day that my son called about a job he had been thinking about for months. He called to join the gym to work out. He became very pleasant to be around and started not only to help around the house, but also to ask what he could do. He has become very social and now I have trouble getting a chance to use the phone. He is going away to look for work with my brother, which would have been unheard of before.

My daughter's attitude also changed. She told me she had talked to a friend long distance with whom the week before she had insisted I had to do the dialing and get her friend on the phone before she would even be in the room. She has been helping and very social.

She had a setback, so I e-mailed Raymon. She had been impossible after school. She came home after school and sat and complained that she just couldn't go to school anymore. She just couldn't do it. I asked what she had to do. She had to write a postcard. She cried for two nights and she had a temperature and was shaking. The day I e-mailed Raymon, he said he adjusted her again and could I let him know how it went. I heard her and a friend coming up the road and she was laughing freely. I asked her how it went. She said she went to the library, did her project, and the teacher said it was great; it was no big deal.

My brother was here because he was so worried about her, asking me what I was going to do with her. I told him she had gotten adjusted again. He is becoming a believer as well, although he is not the type to believe in anything of this nature. Things are going very well here with the kids now and I am so grateful to Raymon. I didn't know where to turn. Conventional therapy may work, but if you have teens who will not go because they are so down and out, what do you do?

Raymon has also done work on me. He adjusted body and prosperity frequencies. I have been working two jobs since his work. I have met a wonderful man, and with the "new" kids, have been amazed at life. Prosperity comes in many disguises.

Thanks so much, Raymon.

It's letters like these that make this work worthwhile. It is appreciative people like this who cause me to want to share this information with others who will use it.

The reference in the letter to the second adjustment Sarah received concerned hormones being out of balance. With the use of the pendulum, I asked to bring Sarah's hormones into total balance.

Here is another story concerning curses.

During a class one day, Carol mentioned that she had a bad right knee. It was swollen and painful, having been that way for years. She also stated that four generations of her family had suffered problems with their right knee. She figured that she just inherited the problem.

I told her, "What you have inherited is four family curses." This came as a surprise, as she had a Ph.D. and her education had not prepared her for such things.

I asked, "Do you want to get rid of them?"

She replied, "Yes, if you know how."

Using the pendulum, I simply asked to neutralize the curses upon the four generations that were affecting her and her family.

Here is a copy of her e-mail two days later.

After class on Saturday, you cleared my right knee of a curse on the family that goes back at least to great-great ancestors. Also cleared a couple of other things from that knee. I know you hear "miraculous" all the time and it was.

I can now walk with the right foot pointing forward in perfect alignment without pain or feeling of strain. I spent Monday through Wednesday painting and going up and down a stepladder. The knee did not swell or become painful. The most amazing thing was that on Tuesday I realized I was actually stepping up with the right leg with complete confidence that it would hold me—a thing I could not do last week! (Tells me the problem wasn't muscular.)

The first thing I noticed, though, was that the right ankle was not swelling during the day. It used to do that whether the knee was actively bothering me or not. *Thanks!*

One last comment. Unlike most workshops where participants come home tired out and put the materials aside for a while, those of us I have been in touch with, who attended your class last weekend in Greensboro, started dowsing and typing notes and other such activities as soon as we got home. And the momentum remains high today. Thanks for your type of healing energy in this world.

Carol

Carol Graybeal Chafin, M.B.A., Ph.D.

Acupressure, dowsing, Healing Touch apprentice, Reiki master teacher

Feedback, Respect, and Attitude

Some healers have a problem getting feedback from those requesting their assistance. One of my healer friends said something like this: "When it comes to getting feedback from a person, you can forget it. After working on them, you will never hear from them again until they have a relative or friend on their deathbed. Then they will call, expecting you to perform a miracle."

I have taken a more hard-line approach. If a person is unwilling to do something for themselves, provide feedback, and compensate me for my time, I'm willing to let them keep their problems.

Once during a talk, a woman in the audience wanted to tell her life story of all the misery, ailments, and long list of doctors and clinics she had been through. She wanted me to take care of all her problems, and she wanted it *now.*

I replied, "You have exhausted most of the healing and medical profession. You still have your problems and you expect a mountain man to fix you immediately?"

She thought my answer was sarcastic. I thought it was realistic. This is not to be taken as a contradiction to statements made in this book concerning random acts of kindness and helping friends. It is simply saying that when a person calls and expects me to stop whatever I'm doing to fix their problem, I expect to be compensated for it. At first I wanted to help as many people as possible and still do.

Some things happened that made me change some of my attitudes. Every night when we sat down to eat, the phone would ring. When I was reading April a bedtime story, the phone would ring. When I was getting ready to go to work, the phone would ring. These calls were from good people with problems, but they wanted me to fix their problems *at their convenience, for free.* After a few years of this, my attitude changed. I decided if these people wanted me to work for them, then they had to offer something in return. If I sound like a mercenary, so be it.

I feel that many healers do not get the respect they deserve and it may be because they don't demand it. Most healers I know are caring and generous with their time and abilities. However, there is an element of people who look down on what we do, perhaps because it isn't accepted by mainstream society.

I have been told, "I'll let the doctors see what they can do, and if they can't help me, then I'll let you try." I tell these people in no uncertain terms that I don't want to work on them and they can keep their problems. I'm not opposed to them going to their doctor. I just don't like their attitude.

Some healers may feel an obligation to work on everyone. May God bless them. I don't feel this way. My friend Rolling Thunder didn't either. He would ask a person what they intended to do with their life if they got well. He didn't think it fair when a person would have all manner of operations, their body filled with drugs and chemicals, each to correct the ill effects of the other, and then come to a healer for help.

Criminals

For some reason, the spirit world seems to have picked me to do some of the dirty work. Why? Probably because I'll do it. One of these jobs has been preventing serial killers from ever killing again. There is no definite proof of this, but the evidence is pretty good. Here is one of the stories as I got it.

If I have kept up with the years correctly, this happened in March of 1996.

A serial killer known as the I-29 Stalker was operating near Charlottesville, Virginia. His method of operation was to drive close behind a lone woman at night and flash his lights repeatedly until she pulled to the side of the road. He would then rape and kill her. There were wanted posters out across the state, but there was no description of him.

My friend Ross, who worked as an undercover agent, came to visit me and asked for help. I was unable to locate the killer, but thought perhaps he could be made harmless. All I knew to do was ask Grandfather if he was able and willing to take the negative entities away from him. The response from Grandfather in the spirit world was, "Yes." It's been five years and there hasn't been another attack after using this method of operation.

(Note: About a year after this was first printed, six years after I worked on the case, there was another attempt, by perhaps the same attacker. This time he failed in his attempt, was identified, and shortly after, killed himself.)

A carnival worker went berserk near where we live and killed three women in a crime spree over a few hundred miles. Again, I was unable to locate him, but was able to de-possess him. De-possessing a person takes a lot of power from them, and in many cases makes them less dangerous.

A few days later, I was talking with a U.S. marshal about the capture of the person. The man was armed and considered extremely dangerous. The marshal couldn't figure out how the killer was captured without resistance. I could.

There have been other instances similar to these and some where we believed someone was prevented from becoming a killer of children. Of course, if someone is not a known killer and never becomes one, it is not provable that such things would have ever happened.

Something has both amazed and disappointed me. There are so few people willing to get involved in the prevention of abuse or serial raping and killing. One summer, there was the opportunity to speak to more than 30 police in a training session. I made them an offer. "With a great degree of success, I can show you how to stop a serial killer from ever killing again. But I won't do it unless you ask."

You know how many asked? One! And he called me aside so no one else would hear. Three of them asked for my card and said if they heard of one, they would call me.

The way I see it is, if we detect such a potential problem, we have a couple of choices. Do nothing or do something. If we do nothing, a lot of needless suffering may take place. If we do something, such suffering may be eliminated. At least we will have the satisfaction of knowing we tried.

In the world of healing, don't expect to be recognized and rewarded for many things you do. You see a situation where something needs to be done, no one else is available to do anything, so you do it and no one ever knows. One of my beliefs is that no act of kindness, regardless of how small, is ever wasted. Being able to offer scientific proof of these things is of little interest to me. It would be OK to have, but probably impossible to obtain.

Just this morning a call was received from the mother of one of my friends. She just wanted to tell me her bottle of arthritis medicine had been untouched since Christmas when I visited and worked with her. She says she hasn't needed it. She doesn't think she has arthritis anymore, and maybe she doesn't. Could we prove my work had anything to do with it? No, but she thinks so. Do I care because it is unprovable? No, what I care about is the fact she doesn't hurt anymore.

Do I expect everyone to believe these past few paragraphs? No, but some will and they will be the ones who will do something, thereby making something happen. That something may very possibly save several families from a lot of grief.

Throughout this book, examples have been given of changing the behavior of people and conditions. If enough people learned to do this, then we could reach what is called "critical mass" and change conditions on the planet. How much does it take to reach critical mass? I don't know. Other writers have given estimates and they may be right. I just know it takes more than we have now.

Raising Earth's Energy

It is now two years after the first printing of this book. Some things have changed—among them, the energy of the Earth and the number of people able to change mass consciousness. What I'm about to write is the way it looks from where I now stand.

In July of 2002 Larry and I were visiting Bill and Winnie Askin, the folks in chapter 8. Bill made a comment concerning a well-known author who had stated something like this: "One percent of the population of the Earth is enough to change mass consciousness."

"Where are we now?" I asked.

"Seven-tenths of a percent" he replied. That is seven people per thousand.

Larry and I figured we might help things along so we started to work on it. About a month later I called to ask Bill.

"Where are we now on the percentage of people who can change mass consciousness?"

"Something seems to have happened, we are now at point-nine-eight percent," he answered.

That is almost 10 people per thousand.

Perhaps it would be appropriate to include some more related information at this time.

In January of 2001 an e-mail was received from Jonna Rae Bartges in San Diego, California. This was someone unknown to me. The letter stated that she had a message from Chief Two Trees to me. The condensed version was that I was to put together a "healing summit" for the Earth in August of 2002.

The farther away the future is, the better it looks, so I said, "OK." I pondered on this for a while and having no idea of how to do it, let it fade from memory.

In mid-August of 2002 Jonna Rae called to ask what I had done concerning the "healing for the Earth."

"Haven't done anything," I told her. "I've been on the road most of the time, don't know where to have it or who to invite. Guess it won't happen."

She suggested using the Internet to put out our message. That hadn't occurred to me.

"How many people can you reach?" I asked.

"Several thousand," she answered.

Within two hours she had been guided to write a request to send to the world, asking people to do whatever they knew how to do, to raise the energy of the Earth, on August 26 at 8 P.M.

We sent it out, people sent it on to others, and so it went. She received responses from people in 13 countries who had participated in the effort.

There were dowsers measuring the energy before and after

the event. At the hour this was done, the energy seemed to rise extremely high and then taper off.

Bill Askin was very excited because the percentage of those able to affect mass consciousness had risen to 1.3. It seemed that humanity had been pushed over the brink on the positive side.

We were so excited about it that we did it again on September 22. By then many other people had become aware of this event and apparently took part in it. This time the percentage of people rose rapidly to six percent in the next few days.

We received comments from people who felt an energy shift at the time the energy was being raised. Some of these knew nothing of our activities but could feel "something happening."

And now, we have done it again on December 22, and according to our dowsing, the percentage has reached a bit over nine percent. It seems that the percentage of people able to raise mass consciousness increased from 0.7 percent to nine percent in four months. This is about 1,280 percent better than humans have done on their own since the beginning of time. A number of factors were involved here but a major one was that one trapper in the bush of Alberta, Canada, taught me how to measure and raise energy.

And now, I have shared this and other information with you. We have only scratched the surface of what is possible with our mind. Today I spoke with Harold McCoy and asked if he has any specific message he would like to put in this book.

His answer was, "Tell them nothing is impossible."

So now, the future really is yours, and you have the information to do something about it. *Make the best of it!*

Pendulum Dowsing Chart

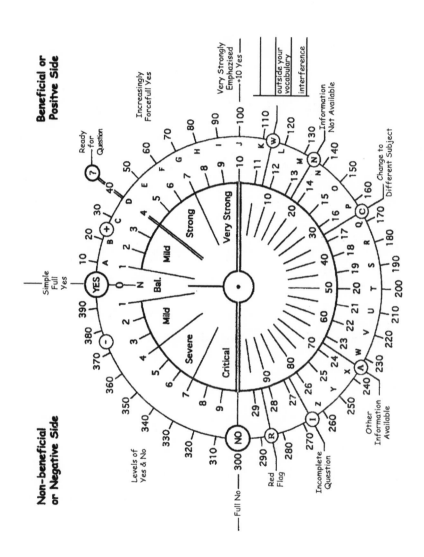

Appendix
The Battle for Your Mind
Persuasion and Brainwashing Techniques Being Used on the Public Today
By Dick Sutphen
serendipity.magnet.ch/sutphen/brainwsh.html

Summary of Contents

Introduction

I'm Dick Sutphen and this tape is a studio-recorded, expanded version of a talk I delivered at the World Congress of Professional Hypnotists Convention in Las Vegas, Nevada. Although the tape carries a copyright to protect it from unlawful duplication for sale by other companies, in this case, I invite individuals to make copies and give them to friends or anyone in a position to communicate this information to others.

Although I've been interviewed about the subject on many local and regional radio and TV talk shows, large-scale mass communication appears to be blocked, since it could result in suspicion or investigation of the very media presenting it or the sponsors that support the media. Some government agencies do not want this information generally known. Nor do the Born-Again Christian movement, cults, and many human-potential trainers.

Everything I will relate exposes only the surface of the problem. I don't know how the misuse of these techniques can be stopped. I don't think it is possible to legislate against that which often cannot be detected; and if those who legislate are using these techniques, there is little hope of affecting laws to govern usage. I do know that the first step to initiate change is to generate interest, which in this case will probably only come from an underground effort.

In talking about this subject, I am talking about my own business. I know it, and I know how effective it can be. I produce hypnosis and subliminal tapes and, in some of my seminars, I use conversion tactics to assist participants to become independent and self-sufficient. But, anytime I use these techniques, I point out that I am using them, and those attending have a choice to participate or not. They also know what the desired result of participation will be.

So, to begin, I want to state the most basic of all facts about brainwashing: In the entire history of man, no one has ever been brainwashed and realized, or believed, that he had been brainwashed. Those who have been brainwashed will usually passionately defend their manipulators, claiming they have simply been "shown the light" . . . or have been transformed in miraculous ways.

The Birth of Conversion: Brainwashing in Christian Revivalism in 1735

Conversion is a nice word for brainwashing . . . and any study of brainwashing has to begin with a study of Christian revivalism in eighteenth-century America. Apparently, Jonathan Edwards accidentally discovered the techniques during a religious crusade in 1735 in Northampton, Massachusetts. By inducing guilt and acute apprehension and by increasing the tension, the "sinners" attending his revival meetings would break down and completely submit. Technically, what Edwards was doing was creating conditions that wipe the brain slate clean so that the mind accepts new programming. The problem was that the new input was negative. He would tell them, "You're a sinner! You're destined for hell!"

As a result, one person committed suicide and another attempted suicide. And the neighbors of the suicidal converts related that they, too, were affected so deeply that, although they had found "eternal salvation," they were obsessed with a diabolical temptation to end their own lives.

Once a preacher, cult leader, manipulator, or authority figure creates the brain phase to wipe the brain slate clean, his subjects are wide open. New input, in the form of suggestion, can be substituted for their previous ideas. Because Edwards didn't turn his message positive until the end of the revival, many accepted the negative suggestions and acted, or desired to act, upon them.

Charles J. Finney was another Christian revivalist who used the same techniques four years later in mass religious conversions in New York. The techniques are still being used today by Christian revivalists, cults, human-potential trainers, some business rallies, and the United States Armed Services . . . to name just a few.

Let me point out here that I don't think most revivalist preachers realize or know they are using brainwashing techniques. Edwards simply stumbled upon a technique that really worked, and others copied it and have continued to copy it for over two hundred years. And the more sophisticated our knowledge and technology has become, the more effective the conversion. I feel strongly that this is one of the major reasons for the increasing rise in Christian fundamentalism, especially the televised variety, while most of the orthodox religions are declining.

The Three Brain Phases: The Pavlovian Explanation

The Christians may have been the first to successfully formulate brainwashing, but we have to look to Pavlov, the Russian scientist, for a technical explanation. In the early 1900s, his work with animals opened the door to further investigations with humans. After the revolution in Russia, Lenin was quick to see the potential of applying Pavlov's research to his own ends.

Three distinct and progressive states of transmarginal inhibition were identified by Pavlov. The first is the equivalent phase, in which the brain gives the same response to both strong and weak stimuli. The second is the paradoxical phase, in which the brain responds more actively to weak stimuli than to strong. And the third is the ultra-paradoxical phase, in which conditioned responses and behavior patterns turn from positive to negative or from negative to positive.

With the progression through each phase, the degree of conversion becomes more effective and complete. The ways to achieve conversion are many and varied, but the usual first step in religious or political brainwashing is to work on the emotions of an individual or group until they reach an abnormal level of anger, fear, excitement, or nervous tension.

The progressive result of this mental condition is to impair judgment and increase suggestibility. The more this condition can be maintained or intensified, the more it compounds. Once catharsis, or the first brain phase, is reached, the complete mental takeover becomes easier. Existing mental programming can be replaced with new patterns of thinking and behavior.

Other often-used physiological weapons to modify normal brain functions are fasting, radical or high-sugar diets, physical discomforts, regulation of breathing, mantra chanting in meditation, the disclosure of awesome mysteries, special lighting and sound effects, programmed response to incense, or intoxicating drugs.

The same results can be obtained in contemporary psychiatric treatment by electric shock treatments and even by purposely lowering a person's blood sugar level with insulin injections.

Before I talk about exactly how some of the techniques are applied, I want to point out that hypnosis and conversion tactics are two distinctly different things—and that conversion techniques are far more powerful. However, the two are often mixed . . . with powerful results.

How Revivalist Preachers Work

If you'd like to see a revivalist preacher at work, there are probably several in your city. Go to the church or tent early and sit in the rear, about three-quarters of the way back. Most likely repetitive music will be played while the people come in for the service. A repetitive beat, ideally ranging from 45 to 72 beats per minute (a rhythm close to the beat of the human heart), is very hypnotic and can generate an eyes-open altered state of consciousness in a very high percentage of people. And, once you are in an alpha state, you are at least 25 times as suggestible as you would be in full beta consciousness. The music is probably the same for every service, or incorporates the same beat, and many of the people will go into an altered state almost immediately upon entering the sanctuary. Subconsciously, they recall their state of mind from previous services and respond according to the post-hypnotic programming.

Watch the people waiting for the service to begin. Many will exhibit external signs of trance—body relaxation and slightly dilated eyes. Often, they begin swaying back and forth with their hands in the air while sitting in their chairs. Next, the assistant pastor will probably come out. He usually speaks with a pretty good "voice roll."

The "Voice Roll" Technique

A "voice roll" is a patterned, paced style used by hypnotists when inducing a trance. It is also used by many lawyers, some of whom are highly trained hypnotists, when they desire to entrench a point firmly in the minds of the jurors. A voice roll can sound as if the speaker were talking to the beat of a metronome or it may sound as though he were emphasizing every word in a monotonous, patterned style. The words will usually be delivered at the rate of 45 to 60 beats per minute, maximizing the hypnotic effect.

The Build-up Process: Inducing Altered States

Now the assistant pastor begins the "build-up" process. He induces an altered state of consciousness and/or begins to generate the excitement and the expectations of the audience. Next, a group of young women in "sweet and pure" chiffon dresses might come out to sing a song. Gospel songs are great for building excitement and involvement. In the middle of the song, one of the girls might be "smitten by the spirit" and fall down or react as if possessed by the Holy Spirit. This very effectively increases the intensity in the room. At this point, hypnosis and conversion tactics are being mixed. And the result is that the audience's attention span is now totally focused upon the communication, while the environment becomes more exciting or tense.

Assured Continuation: Fleecing the Flock

Right about this time, when an eyes-open, mass-induced alpha mental state has been achieved, the collection plate or basket is usually passed. In the background, a 45-beat-per-minute voice roll from the assistant preacher might exhort, "Give to God . . . Give to God . . . Give to God. . . ."

And the audience does give. God may not get the money, but his already-wealthy representative will.

Bonding by Fear and Suggestion

Next, the fire-and-brimstone preacher will come out. He induces fear and increases the tension by talking about "the devil," "going to hell," or the forthcoming Armageddon.

In the last such rally I attended, the preacher talked about the blood that would soon be running out of every faucet in the land. He was also obsessed with a "bloody axe of God," which everyone had seen hanging above the pulpit the previous week. I have no doubt that everyone saw it—the power of suggestion given to hundreds of people in hypnosis assures that at least 10 to 25 percent would see whatever he suggested they see.

Testimony: Creating Community Spirit

In most revivalist gatherings, "testifying" or "witnessing" usually follows the fear-based sermon. People from the audience come up on stage and relate their stories. "I was crippled and now I can walk!" "I had arthritis and now it's gone!" It is a psychological manipulation that works. After listening to numerous case histories of miraculous healings, the average guy in the audience with a minor problem is sure he can be healed. The room is charged with fear, guilt, intense excitement, and expectations.

Miracles

Now those who want to be healed are frequently lined up around the edge of the room, or they are told to come down to the front. The preacher might touch them on the head firmly and scream, "Be healed!" This releases the psychic energy and, for many, catharsis results. Catharsis is a purging of repressed emotions. Individuals might cry, fall down, or even go into spasms. And if catharsis is effected, they stand a chance of being healed. In catharsis (one of the three brain phases mentioned earlier), the brain slate is temporarily wiped clean and the new suggestion is accepted.

For some, the healing may be permanent. For many, it will last four days to a week, which is, incidentally, how long a hypnotic suggestion given to a somnambulistic subject will usually last. Even if the healing doesn't last, if they come back every week, the power of suggestion may continually override the problem . . . or sometimes, sadly, it can mask a physical problem that could prove to be very detrimental to the individual in the long run.

The Grey Area of Legitimacy

I'm not saying that legitimate healings do not take place. They do. Maybe the individual was ready to let go of the negativity that caused the problem in the first place; maybe it was the work of God. Yet I contend that it can be explained with existing knowledge of brain/mind function.

A Game in Which the Rules Keep Changing

The techniques and staging will vary from church to church. Many use "speaking in tongues" to generate catharsis in some, while the spectacle creates intense excitement in the observers.

The use of hypnotic techniques by religions is sophisticated, and professionals are assuring that they become even more effective. A man in Los Angeles is designing, building, and reworking a lot of churches around the country. He tells ministers what they need and how to use it. This man's track record indicates that the congregation and the monetary income will double if the minister follows his instructions. He admits that about 80 percent of his efforts are in the sound system and lighting.

Powerful sound and the proper use of lighting are of primary importance in inducing an altered state of consciousness—I've been using them for years in my own seminars. However, my participants are fully aware of the process and what they can expect as a result of their participation.

Six Conversion Techniques

Cults and human-potential organizations are always looking for new converts. To attain them, they must also create a brainphase. And they often need to do it within a short space of time—a weekend, or maybe even a day. The following are the six primary techniques used to generate the conversion:

Isolation, Intimidation, Deprivation, and Indoctrination

The meeting or training takes place in an area where participants are cut off from the outside world. This may be any place: a private home, a remote or rural setting, or even a hotel ballroom where the participants are allowed only limited bathroom usage. In human-potential trainings, the controllers will give a lengthy talk about the importance of "keeping agreements" in life. The participants are told that if they don't keep agreements, their life will never work. It's a good idea to keep agreements, but the controllers are subverting a positive human value for selfish purposes. The participants vow to themselves and their trainer that they will keep their agreements. Anyone who does not will be intimidated into agreement or forced to leave. The next step is to agree to complete training, thus assuring a high percentage of conversions for the organizations.

They will usually have to agree not to take drugs, smoke, and sometimes not to eat . . . or they are given such short meal breaks that it creates tension. The real reason for the agreements is to alter internal chemistry, which generates anxiety and hopefully causes at least a slight malfunction of the nervous system, which in turn increases the conversion potential.

The "Sell It by Zealot" Technique

Before the gathering is complete, the agreements will be used to ensure that the new converts go out and find new participants. They are intimidated into agreeing to do so before they leave. Since the importance of keeping agreements is so high on their priority list, the converts will twist the arms of everyone they know, attempting to talk them into attending a free introductory session offered at a future date by the organization. The new converts are zealots. In fact, the inside term for merchandising the largest and most successful human-potential training is, "Sell it by zealot!"

At least a million people are graduates and a good percentage have been left with a mental activation button that assures their future loyalty and assistance if the guru figure or organization calls. Think about the potential political implications of hundreds of thousands of zealots programmed to campaign for their guru.

Be wary of an organization of this type that offers follow-up sessions after the seminar. Follow-up sessions might be weekly meetings or inexpensive seminars given on a regular basis, which the organization will attempt to talk you into taking, or any regularly scheduled event used to maintain control. As the early Christian revivalists found, long-term control is dependent upon a good follow-up system.

Wearing Down Resistance

All right. Now, let's look at the second tip-off that indicates conversion tactics are being used. A schedule is maintained that causes physical and mental fatigue. This is primarily accomplished by long hours in which the participants are given no opportunity for relaxation or reflection.

Increasing Tension

The third tip-off: techniques used to increase the tension in the room or environment.

Introducing Uncertainty about Identity

Number four: Uncertainty. I could spend hours relating various techniques to increase tension and generate uncertainty. Basically, the participants are concerned about being "put on the spot" by the trainers, guilt feelings are played upon, participants are tempted to verbally relate their innermost secrets to the other participants, or forced to take part in activities that emphasize removing their masks. One of the most successful human-potential seminars forces the participants to stand on a stage in front of the entire audience while being verbally attacked by the trainers. A public opinion poll, conducted a few years ago, showed that the number one most-fearful situation an individual could encounter is to speak to an audience. It ranked above window washing outside the 85th floor of an office building.

So you can imagine the fear and tension this situation generates within the participants. Many faint, but most cope with the stress by mentally going away. They literally go into an alpha state, which automatically makes them many times as suggestible as they normally are. And another loop of the downward spiral into conversion is successfully effected.

Jargon

The fifth clue that conversion tactics are being used is the introduction of jargon—new terms that have meaning only to the "insiders" who participate. Vicious language is also frequently used, purposely, to make participants uncomfortable.

Lack of Humor: No Release, No Resistance

The final tip-off is that there is no humor in the communications . . . at least until the participants are converted. Then, merry-making and humor are highly desirable as symbols of the new joy the participants have supposedly "found."

Not Always a Bad Thing

I'm not saying that good does not result from participation in such gatherings. It can and does. But I contend it is important for people to know what has happened and to be aware that continual involvement may not be in their best interest.

Over the years, I've conducted professional seminars to teach people to be hypnotists, trainers, and counselors. I've had many of those who conduct trainings and rallies come to me and say, "I'm here because I know that what I'm doing works, but I don't know why." After showing them how and why, many have gotten out of the business or have decided to approach it differently or in a much more loving and supportive manner.

Many of these trainers have become personal friends, and it

scares us all to have experienced the power of one person with a microphone and a room full of people. Add a little charisma and you can count on a high percentage of conversions. The sad truth is that a high percentage of people want to give away their power—they are true "believers"!

Cults: A Captive Course in Stockholm Syndrome

Cult gatherings or human-potential trainings are an ideal environment to observe firsthand what is technically called the "Stockholm Syndrome." This is a situation in which those who are intimidated, controlled, or made to suffer, begin to love, admire, and even sometimes sexually desire their controllers or captors.

But let me inject a word of warning here: if you think you can attend such gatherings and not be affected, you are probably wrong. A perfect example is the case of a woman who went to Haiti on a Guggenheim Fellowship to study Haitian voodoo. In her report, she related how the music eventually induced uncontrollable bodily movement and an altered state of consciousness. Although she understood the process and thought herself above it, when she began to feel herself become vulnerable to the music, she attempted to fight it and turned away. Anger or resistance almost always ensures conversion. A few moments later she was possessed by the music and began dancing in a trance around the voodoo meeting house. A brain-phase had been induced by the music and excitement, and she awoke feeling reborn.

The Only Hope of Immunity

The only hope of attending such gatherings without being affected is to be a Buddha and allow no positive or negative emotions to surface. Few people are capable of such detachment.

The U.S. Marines As a Brainwashing Cult

Before I go on, let's go back to the six tip-offs to conversion. I want to mention the United States Government and military boot camp. The Marine Corps talks about breaking men down before "rebuilding" them as new men—as marines! Well, that is exactly what they do, the same way a cult breaks its people down and rebuilds them as happy flower sellers on your local street corner. Every one of the six conversion techniques is used in boot camp. Considering the needs of the military, I'm not making a judgment as to whether that is good or bad. *It is a fact* that the men are effectively brainwashed. Those who won't submit must be discharged or spend much of their time in the brig.

Steps in the Decognition Process

Once the initial conversion is effected, cults, armed services, and similar groups cannot have cynicism among their members. Members must respond to commands and do as they are told, otherwise they are dangerous to the organizational control. This is normally accomplished as a three-step decognition process.

Alertness Reduction

Step 1 is alertness reduction: The controllers cause the nervous system to malfunction, making it difficult to distinguish between fantasy and reality. This can be accomplished in several ways. Poor diet is one; watch out for brownies and Kool-Aid. The sugar throws the nervous system off. More subtle is the "spiritual diet" used by many cults. They eat only vegetables and fruits; without the grounding of grains, nuts, seeds, dairy products, fish, or meat, an individual becomes mentally "spacey." Inadequate sleep is another primary way to reduce alertness, especially when combined with long hours of work or intense physical activity. Also, being bombarded with intense and unique experiences achieves the same result.

Programmed Confusion

Step 2 is programmed confusion: You are mentally assaulted while your alertness is being reduced as in step 1. This is accomplished with a deluge of new information, lectures, discussion groups, encounters, or one-to-one processing, which usually amounts to the controller bombarding the individual with questions. During this phase of decognition, reality and illusion often merge and perverted logic is likely to be accepted.

Thought Stopping

Step 3 is thought stopping: Techniques are used to cause the mind to go "flat." These are altered-state-of-consciousness techniques that initially induce calmness by giving the mind something simple to deal with and then focusing awareness. The continued use brings on a feeling of elation and eventually hallucination. The result is the reduction of thought and eventually, if used long enough, the cessation of all thought and withdrawal from everyone and everything except that which the controllers direct. The takeover is then complete. It is important to be aware that when members or participants are instructed to use "thought-stopping" techniques, they are told that they will benefit by so doing: they will become "better soldiers" or "find enlightenment."

Thought-Stopping Techniques

Marching

There are three primary techniques used for thought stopping. The first is marching: the thump, thump, thump beat literally generates self-hypnosis and thus great susceptibility to suggestion.

Meditation

The second thought-stopping technique is meditation. If you spend an hour to an hour and a half a day in meditation, after a few weeks, there is a great probability that you will not return to full beta consciousness. You will remain in a fixed state of alpha for as long as you continue to meditate. I'm not saying this is bad—if you do it yourself. It may be very beneficial. But it is a fact that you are causing your mind to go flat. I've worked with meditators on an EEG machine and the results are conclusive: the more you meditate, the flatter your mind becomes until, eventually, and especially if used to excess or in combination with decognition, all thought ceases. Some spiritual groups see this as nirvana—which is bullshit. It is simply a predictable physiological result. And if Heaven on Earth is a state of non-thinking and non-involvement, I really question why we are here.

Chanting

The third thought-stopping technique is chanting, and often chanting in meditation. "Speaking in tongues" could also be included in this category.

All three thought-stopping techniques produce an altered state of consciousness. This may be very good if you are controlling the process, for you also control the input. I personally use at least one self-hypnosis programming session every day and I know how beneficial it is for me. But you need to know if you use these techniques to the degree of remaining continually in alpha that, although you'll be very mellow, you'll also be more suggestible.

True Believers and Mass Movements

Before ending this section on conversion, I want to talk about the people who are most susceptible to it and about mass movements. I am convinced that at least a third of the population are what Eric Hoffer calls "true believers." They are joiners and followers—people who want to give away their power. They look for answers, meaning, and enlightenment outside themselves.

Hoffer, who wrote *The True Believer*, a classic on mass movements, says, "True believers are not intent on bolstering and advancing a cherished self, but are those craving to be rid of unwanted self. They are followers, not because of a desire for self-advancement, but because it can satisfy their passion for self-renunciation!" Hoffer also says that true believers "are eternally incomplete and eternally insecure!"

I know this from my own experience. In my years of communicating concepts and conducting trainings, I have run into them again and again. All I can do is attempt to show them that the only thing to seek is the True Self within. Their personal answers are to be found there and there alone. I communicate that the basics of spirituality are self-responsibility and self-actualization. But most of the true believers just tell me that I'm not spiritual and go looking for someone who will give them the dogma and structure they desire.

Never underestimate the potential danger of these people. They can easily be molded into fanatics who will gladly work and die for their holy cause. It is a substitute for their lost faith in themselves and offers them a substitute for individual hope. The Moral Majority is made up of true believers. All cults are composed of true believers. You'll find them in politics, churches, businesses, and social cause groups. They are the fanatics in these organizations.

Mass movements will usually have a charismatic leader. The followers want to convert others to their way of living or impose a new way of life—if necessary, by legislating laws forcing others to their view, as evidenced by the activities of the Moral

Majority. This means enforcement by guns or punishment, for that is the bottom-line in law enforcement.

A common hatred, enemy, or devil is essential to the success of a mass movement. The Born-Again Christians have Satan himself, but that isn't enough—they've added the occult, the New Age thinkers and, lately, all those who oppose the integration of church and politics, as evidenced in their political reelection campaigns against those who oppose their views. In revolutions, the devil is usually the ruling power or aristocracy. Some human-potential movements are far too clever to ask their graduates to join anything, thus labeling themselves as a cult—but, if you look closely, you'll find that their devil is anyone and everyone who hasn't taken their training.

There are mass movements without devils but they seldom attain major status. The true believers are mentally unbalanced or insecure people, or those without hope or friends. People don't look for allies when they love, but they do when they hate or become obsessed with a cause. And those who desire a new life and a new order feel the old ways must be eliminated before the new order can be built.

Persuasion Techniques

Persuasion isn't technically brainwashing, but it is the manipulation of the human mind by another individual, without the manipulated party being aware what caused his opinion shift. I only have time to very basically introduce you to a few of the thousands of techniques in use today, but the basis of persuasion is always to access your right brain. The left half of your brain is analytical and rational. The right side is creative and imaginative. That is overly simplified but it makes my point. So, the idea is to distract the left brain and keep it busy. Ideally, the persuader generates an eyes-open altered state of consciousness, causing you to shift from beta awareness into alpha; this can be measured on an EEG machine.

"Yes Set"

First, let me give you an example of distracting the left brain. Politicians use these powerful techniques all the time; lawyers use many variations which, I've been told, they call "tightening the noose."

Assume for a moment that you are watching a politician give a speech. First, he might generate what is called a "yes set." These are statements that will cause listeners to agree; they might even unknowingly nod their heads in agreement. Next come the truisms. These are usually facts that could be debated but, once the politician has his audience agreeing, the odds are in the politician's favor that the audience won't stop to think for themselves, thus continuing to agree. Last comes the suggestion. This is what the politician wants you to do and, since you have been agreeing all along, you could be persuaded to accept the suggestion. Now, if you'll listen closely to my political speech, you'll find that the first three are the "yes set," the next three are truisms, and the last is the suggestion.

Ladies and gentlemen: Are you angry about high food prices? Are you tired of astronomical gas prices? Are you sick of out-of-control inflation? Well, you know the Other Party allowed 18 percent inflation last year, you know crime has increased 50 percent nationwide in the last 12 months, and you know your paycheck hardly covers your expenses any more. Well, the answer to resolving these problems is to elect me, John Jones, to the U.S. Senate.

Embedded Commands

And I think you've heard all that before. But you might also watch for what are called embedded commands. As an example:

On key words, the speaker would make a gesture with his left hand, which research has shown is more apt to access your right brain. Today's media-oriented politicians and spellbinders are often carefully trained by a whole new breed of specialists who are using every trick in the book—both old and new— to manipulate you into accepting their candidate.

The Power of NLP

The concepts and techniques of Neuro-Linguistics are so heavily protected that I found out the hard way that to even talk about them publicly or in print results in threatened legal action. Yet Neuro-Linguistic training is readily available to anyone willing to devote the time and pay the price. It is some of the most subtle and powerful manipulation I have yet been exposed to. A good friend who recently attended a two-week seminar on Neuro-Linguistics found that many of those she talked to during the breaks were government people.

Interspersal Technique

Another technique that I'm just learning about is unbelievably slippery; it is called an interspersal technique and the idea is to say one thing with words but plant a subconscious impression of something else in the minds of the listeners and/or watchers.

PRACTICAL EXAMPLES

Let me give you an example. Assume you are watching a television commentator make the following statement: "Senator Johnson is assisting local authorities to clear up the stupid mistakes of companies contributing to the nuclear waste problems." It sounds like a statement of fact, but, if the speaker emphasizes the right word, and especially if he makes the proper hand gestures on the key words, you could be left with the subconscious impression that Senator Johnson is stupid. That was the subliminal goal of the statement and the speaker cannot be called to account for anything.

Persuasion techniques are also frequently used on a much smaller scale with just as much effectiveness. The insurance salesman knows his pitch is likely to be much more effective if he can get you to visualize something in your mind. This is right-brain communication. For instance, he might pause in his conversation, look slowly around your living room and say, "Can you just imagine this beautiful home burning to the ground?" Of course you can! It is one of your unconscious fears and when he forces you to visualize it, you are more likely to be manipulated into signing his insurance policy.

Shock and Confusion

The Hare Krishnas, operating in every airport, use what I call shock and confusion techniques to distract the left brain and communicate directly with the right brain. While waiting for a plane, I once watched one operate for over an hour. He had a technique of almost jumping in front of someone. Initially, his voice was loud then dropped as he made his pitch to take a book and contribute money to the cause. Usually, when people are shocked, they immediately withdraw. In this case they were shocked by the strange appearance, sudden materialization, and loud voice of the Hare Krishna devotee. In other words, the people went into an alpha state for security because they didn't want to confront the reality before them.

In alpha, they were highly suggestible so they responded to the suggestion of taking the book; the moment they took the book, they felt guilty and responded to the second suggestion—give money. We are all conditioned that if someone gives us something, we have to give them something in return—in that case, it was money. While watching this hustler, I was close enough to notice that many of the people he stopped exhibited an outward sign of alpha—their eyes were actually dilated.

Subliminal Programming

Subliminals are hidden suggestions that only your subconscious perceives. They can be audio (hidden behind music), or visual (airbrushed into a picture, flashed on a screen so fast that you don't consciously see them, or cleverly incorporated into a picture or design).

Most audio subliminal reprogramming tapes offer verbal suggestions recorded at a low volume. I question the efficacy of this technique—if subliminals are not perceptible, they cannot be effective, and subliminals recorded below the audible threshold are therefore useless. The oldest audio subliminal technique uses a voice that follows the volume of the music so subliminals are impossible to detect without a parametric equalizer. But this technique is patented and, when I wanted to develop my own line of subliminal audiocassettes, negotiations with the patent holder proved to be unsatisfactory.

My attorney obtained copies of the patents, which I gave to some talented Hollywood sound engineers, asking them to create a new technique. They found a way to psycho-acoustically modify and synthesize the suggestions so that they are projected in the same chord and frequency as the music, thus giving them the effect of being part of the music. But we found that in using this technique, there is no way to reduce various frequencies to detect the subliminals. In other words, although the suggestions are being heard by the subconscious mind, they cannot be monitored with even the most sophisticated equipment.

If we were able to come up with this technique as easily as we did, I can only imagine how sophisticated the technology has become, with unlimited government or advertising funding. And I shudder to think about the propaganda and commercial manipulation that we are exposed to on a daily basis. There is simply no way to know what is behind the music you hear. It may even be possible to hide a second voice behind the voice to which you are listening.

The series by Wilson Bryan Key, Ph.D., on subliminals in advertising and political campaigns well documents the misuse in many areas, especially printed advertising in newspapers, magazines, and posters.

DOES SUBLIMINAL PROGRAMMING WORK?

The big question about subliminals is: do they work? And I guarantee you they do. Not only from the response of those who have used my tapes, but from the results of such programs as the subliminals behind the music in department stores. Supposedly, the only message is instructions to not steal: one East Coast department store chain reported a 37 percent reduction in thefts in the first nine months of testing.

A 1984 article in the technical newsletter, "Brain-Mind Bulletin," states that as much as 99 percent of our cognitive activity may be "non-conscious," according to the director of the Laboratory for Cognitive Psychophysiology at the University of Illinois. The lengthy report ends with the statement, "These findings support the use of subliminal approaches such as taped suggestions for weight loss and the therapeutic use of hypnosis and Neuro-Linguistic Programming."

MASS MISUSE OF SUBLIMINAL PROGRAMMING

I could relate many stories that support subliminal programming, but I'd rather use my time to make you aware of even more subtle uses of such programming.

I have personally experienced sitting in a Los Angeles auditorium with over ten thousand people who were gathered to listen to a current charismatic figure. Twenty minutes after entering the auditorium, I became aware that I was going in and out of an altered state. Those accompanying me experienced the same thing. Since it is our business, we were aware of what was happening, but those around us were not. By careful observation, what appeared to be spontaneous demonstrations were, in fact, artful manipulations. The only way I could figure that the eyes-open trance had been induced was that a 6- to 7-cycle-per-second vibration was being piped into the room behind the air conditioner sound. That particular vibration generates alpha, which would render the audience highly susceptible. Ten to 25 percent of the population is capable of a somnambulistic level of altered states of consciousness; for these people, the suggestions of the speaker, if non-threatening, could potentially be accepted as "commands."

Vibrato

This leads to the mention of vibrato. Vibrato is the tremulous effect imparted in some vocal or instrumental music, and the cycle-per-second range causes people to go into an altered state of consciousness. At one period of English history, singers whose voices contained pronounced vibrato were not allowed to perform publicly because listeners would go into an altered state and have fantasies, often sexual in nature.

People who attend opera or enjoy listening to singers like Mario Lanza are familiar with this altered state induced by the performers.

Extra-low Frequency Vibrations (ELFs)

Now, let's carry this awareness a little farther. There are also inaudible ELFs (extra-low frequency waves). These are electromagnetic in nature. One of the primary uses of ELFs is to communicate with our submarines. Dr. Andrija Puharich, a highly respected researcher, in an attempt to warn U.S. officials about Russian use of ELFs, set up an experiment. Volunteers were wired so their brain waves could be measured on an EEG. They were sealed in a metal room that could not be penetrated by a normal signal.

Puharich then beamed ELF waves at the volunteers. ELFs go right through the earth and, of course, right through metal walls. Those inside couldn't know if the signal was or was not being sent. And Puharich watched the reactions on the technical equipment: 30 percent of those inside the room were taken over by the ELF signal in six to ten seconds.

When I say "taken over," I mean that their behavior followed the changes anticipated at very precise frequencies. Waves below 6 cycles per second caused the subjects to become very emotionally upset, and even disrupted bodily functions. At 8.2 cycles, they felt very high . . . an elevated feeling, as though they had been in masterful meditation, learned over a period of years. Eleven to 11.3 cycles induced waves of depressed agitation leading to riotous behavior.

The Neurophone

Dr. Patrick Flanagan is a personal friend of mine. In the early 1960s, as a teenager, Pat was listed as one of the top scientists in the world by *Life* magazine. Among his many inventions was a device he called the Neurophone—an electronic instrument that can successfully program suggestions directly through contact with the skin. When he attempted to patent the device, the government demanded that he prove it worked. When he did, the National Security Agency confiscated the neurophone. It took Pat two years of legal battle to get his invention back.

In using the device, you don't hear or see a thing; it is applied to the skin, which Pat claims is the source of special senses. The skin contains more sensors for heat, touch, pain, vibration, and electrical fields than any other part of the human anatomy.

In one of his recent tests, Pat conducted two identical seminars for a military audience—one seminar one night and one the next night, because the size of the room was not large enough to accommodate all of them at one time. When the first group proved to be very cool and unwilling to respond, Patrick spent the next day making a special tape to play at the second seminar. The tape instructed the audience to be extremely warm and responsive and for their hands to become "tingly." The tape was played through the neurophone, which was connected to a wire he placed along the ceiling of the room. There were no speakers, so no sound could be heard, yet the message was successfully transmitted from that wire directly into the brains of the audience. They were warm and receptive, their hands tingled and they responded, according to programming, in other ways that I cannot mention here.

Technological Tools for Mass Manipulation

The more we find out about how human beings work through today's highly advanced technological research, the more we learn to control human beings. And what probably scares me the most is that the medium for takeover is already in place. The television set in your living room and bedroom is doing a lot more than just entertaining you.

Before I continue, let me point out something else about an altered state of consciousness. When you go into an altered state, you transfer into right brain, which results in the internal release of the body's own opiates—enkephalins and Beta-endorphins, chemically almost identical to opium. In other words, it feels good . . . and you want to come back for more.

Recent tests by researcher Herbert Krugman showed that, while viewers were watching TV, right-brain activity outnumbered left-brain activity by a ratio of two to one. Put more simply, the viewers were in an altered state . . . in trance more often than not. They were getting their Beta-endorphin "fix."

To measure attention spans, psychophysiologist Thomas Mulholland of the Veterans Hospital in Bedford, Massachusetts, attached young viewers to an EEG machine that was wired to shut the TV set off whenever the children's brains produced a majority of alpha waves. Although the children were told to concentrate, only a few could keep the set on for more than 30 seconds!

Most viewers are already hypnotized. To deepen the trance is easy. One simple way is to place a blank, black frame every 32 frames in the film that is being projected. This creates a 45-beat-per-minute pulsation perceived only by the subconscious mind—the ideal pace to generate deep hypnosis.

The commercials or suggestions presented following this alpha-inducing broadcast are much more likely to be accepted by the viewer. The high percentage of the viewing audience that has somnambulistic-depth ability could very well accept the suggestions as commands—as long as those commands did not ask the viewer to do something contrary to his morals, religion, or self-preservation.

The medium for takeover is here. By the age of 16, children have spent 10,000 to 15,000 hours watching television—that is more time than they spend in school! In the average home, the TV set is on for six hours and 44 minutes per day—an increase of nine minutes from last year and three times the average rate of increase during the 1970s.

It obviously isn't getting better . . . we are rapidly moving into an alpha-level world—very possibly the Orwellian world of 1984—placid, glassy-eyed, and responding obediently to instructions.

A research project by Jacob Jacoby, a Purdue University psychologist, found that of 2,700 people tested, 90 percent misunderstood even such simple viewing fare as commercials and "Barnaby Jones." Only minutes after watching, the typical viewer missed 23 to 36 percent of the questions about what he or she had seen. Of course they did—they were going in and out of trance! If you go into a deep trance, you must be instructed to remember—otherwise you automatically forget.

In Closing ...

I have just touched the tip of the iceberg. When you start to combine subliminal messages behind the music, subliminal visuals projected on the screen, hypnotically produced visual effects, sustained musical beats at a trance-inducing pace ... you have extremely effective brainwashing. Every hour that you spend watching the TV set you become more conditioned. And, in case you thought there was a law against any of these things, guess again. There isn't! There are a lot of powerful people who obviously prefer things exactly the way they are. Maybe they have plans for *you*?

Modified for WWW distribution May 27, 1995, by Dynamic Living Media. May be freely copied and reproduced, complete with all graphics. Neither the editor nor the publisher knows the current whereabouts of Dick Sutphen. Please conduct searches for the author through the usual channels. Last modified: September 23, 1995.

Acknowledgment of the Source of this Document

The author has given permission for this document to be distributed without change. It was obtained from The Psycho-babble Cafe, a site that has now disappeared. The article has since reappeared on Dick Sutphen's web site at https://richardsutphen.com/free

Other articles by Dick Sutphen are also available there.

About the Author

 Raymon Grace, founder and president of Raymon Grace Foundation, is a dowser, lecturer and author of three books, *The Future is Yours, Techniques That Work For Me,* and *Seasons of April.* He has created forty DVDs sharing information learned over the past forty years. His books have all been printed in both English and Chinese. His work is being used in several countries for improving water and self-improvement. His films have reached people in 142 countries. He has been a guest on numerous radio talk shows including the well-known "Coast to Coast AM Radio."

Raymon Grace is a down-to-earth, plain-spoken person who tells it as he sees it. His dress clothes are jeans and cowboy boots, and he doesn't own a suit and tie. He's real.

Hampton Roads Publishing Company

... *for the evolving human spirit*

Hampton Roads Publishing Company
publishes books on a variety of subjects,
including spirituality, health,
and other related topics.

For a copy of our latest trade catalog, call (978) 465-0504 or
visit our distributor's website at *www.redwheelweiser.com*.
You can also sign up for our newsletter and special offers by
going to *www.redwheelweiser.com/newsletter/*.